SELF-PUBLISHING TO AMAZON KDP IN 2025

A BEGINNER'S GUIDE TO SELLING E-BOOKS, AUDIOBOOKS & PAPERBACKS ON AMAZON, AUDIBLE & BEYOND

BRIAN CHESSON

Copyright © 2025 Brian Chesson

All rights reserved. No part of this publication may be reproduced, distributed or transmitted in any form or by any means, including photocopying, recording, or other electronic or mechanical methods, without the prior written permission of the publisher, except in the case of brief quotations embodied in critical reviews and certain other non-commercial uses permitted by copyright law.

Trademarked names appear throughout this book. Rather than use a trademark symbol with every occurrence of a trademarked name, names are used in an editorial fashion, with no intention of infringement of the respective owner's trademark. The information in this book is distributed on an "as is" basis, without warranty. Although every precaution has been taken in the preparation of this work, neither the author nor the publisher shall have any liability to any person or entity with respect to any loss or damage caused or alleged to be caused directly or indirectly by the information contained in this book.

CONTENTS

Intro	v
1. The Beginning	1
2. Self-Publishing vs Traditional Publishing	3
3. What Do You Publish?	7
4. Keywords	11
5. Enrolling in KDP Select	27
6. Pen Names	31
7. Book Ideation & Outlines	35
8. Getting Started with Your First Book	43
9. Images and Illustrations	47
10. Polishing Your Manuscript	53
11. Formatting Your Book	57
12. Setting Up Your KDP Account	61
13. Formatting Your Book Files for Upload	67
14. Designing Your Book Cover	71
15. Uploading Your eBook	83
16. Uploading Your Paperback	101
17. Getting Reviews for Your Book	107
18. Audiobooks	117
19. Pricing Your Books	127
20. Marketing & Social Media	131
21. Amazon Ads for Authors	135
22. Conclusion	143
23. All Links	147

INTRO

Let's get one thing out of the way—you might notice this book isn't hundreds of pages long. That's by design. I didn't pad it with filler or fluff just to hit some imaginary page count. Instead, I've distilled everything down to what actually matters, guiding you from point A to point B as efficiently as possible. You can finish this book in under two hours and walk away with practical, actionable insights you can apply immediately.

Don't judge its value by the page count. Every paragraph is packed with hard-earned lessons from years of building a successful KDP business. I'm not here to waste your time—I'm here to accelerate your results.

Now, you might be wondering: *Why give all this away? What's in it for you?* Here's the truth: I've learned that an abundance mindset always wins. The more I share, the more opportunity flows back. And if this book helps someone else level up—whether that's you, my brother, or my cousin—it's worth it.

This model has changed my life. I've tested countless side hustles and businesses over the years, but I keep coming back to KDP. There's nothing else quite like it. So think of this book as both a blueprint and a gift—one that I wish I had when I started.

Before we dive in, just two quick notes: All prices are listed in U.S. dollars, and every resource or link mentioned in the book is compiled at the end for easy access. Let's get started.

1
THE BEGINNING

Imagine this: it's 2018, and I'm back home, flat broke after an unforgettable year of backpacking across Europe. With my bank account in the red and my wanderlust still buzzing, I found myself doing what any desperate millennial does—scrolling through YouTube for side hustle ideas. That's when I stumbled across this guy, Stephan James, preaching the gospel of Kindle Direct Publishing (KDP). According to him, you can write a book, slap it on Amazon, and watch the passive income roll in. Sounded too good to be true, but I figured, why not give it a shot?

I dove headfirst into the rabbit hole, watching hours of videos and fully expecting to uncover a scam. But to my surprise, the content made sense. The strategies were logical. I figured, "What do I have to lose? A little time?"

So I took the first step Stephan recommended: write about something you know inside-out. At the time, I was deep into growing and selling Instagram accounts. I knew the ins and outs cold. Within a week, I had 10,000 words typed up—2,000 a day, no problem.

I designed the cover myself on Canva. Formatted the book in Google Docs. Uploaded everything to KDP. And just like that, within 24 hours, my eBook and paperback were live on Amazon. The next day? My first royalty: $2. And it felt like a million. I remember thinking, *Wait a second... this actually works?*

That was the moment everything changed. I set a goal: $2,000/month. It felt huge at the time. I assumed I'd need to publish hundreds of books to get there. But here's the twist—I didn't.

In just a few months, with only about two dozen books, I was earning that $2,000 a month. Fast forward to today, and this little experiment has grown into a full-time publishing business pulling in over $10,000 every single month.

Here's the lesson: you don't need a massive catalog to succeed. You just need the right strategy, executed well.

So now, seven years later, I'm pulling back the curtain. If I were starting from scratch in 2025, this is exactly how I'd do it.

2

SELF-PUBLISHING VS TRADITIONAL PUBLISHING

Why Self-Publish?

Let's be honest—do you know how to land a traditional publishing deal? Neither do I. And from what I've heard from those who've been through it, the process is long, exhausting, and often ends with authors resenting the very book they poured their heart into.

The payout? Not worth it. Most traditionally published authors earn around 10% of each book sale—and that's after the publisher takes their cut. Worse still, many authors discover too late that traditional publishers don't do much marketing. You're still expected to promote the book yourself.

Now compare that with self-publishing on Amazon: you earn up to 60% royalty on paperbacks (after printing costs) and 70% on eBooks priced between $2.99 and $9.99. That means if you sell a paperback for $14.99, you'll keep about $6. Sell an eBook for $2.99, and you pocket roughly $2. (Quick note: large eBook files—especially those with lots of images—may incur a small delivery fee that slightly reduces your royalty.)

Sure, traditional publishers will handle the cover design and formatting for you, but at what cost? With self-publishing, you keep control. There are no deadlines. No gatekeepers. You move at your own pace.

And don't worry—I'll show you exactly how to find great designers, formatters, and other freelancers to help you produce a professional book without relying on a publisher.

Should I Only Publish on Amazon?

In short, yes.

Amazon dominates the book market. It accounts for nearly half of all print book sales and over 70% of eBook sales globally. And it's not just the U.S.—they're present in countries like the U.K., Canada, Australia, Germany, Japan, Italy, and more. New marketplaces are being added regularly (Poland joined recently), which means your book can reach readers across the world with a single upload.

That's the beauty of Amazon: you publish once, and they handle the rest—printing, shipping, digital delivery, customer service, and international reach. No juggling multiple platforms. No need to learn new systems. You focus on creating, and Amazon takes care of distribution.

Still need more convincing? Let me introduce you to a concept that has guided much of my business thinking: Pareto's Principle, also known as the 80/20 rule. It suggests that roughly 80% of your results come from 20% of your actions. Whether it's 70/30 or even 90/10, the idea holds: a small portion of your effort delivers most of your income.

When it comes to publishing, Amazon is that 20%. Upload your book, optimize it, then move on to the next one. You'll earn the bulk of your revenue here without spreading yourself thin. Trying to squeeze out the remaining 20% of potential earnings from other platforms often requires 80% more work—setting up new accounts, learning new systems, formatting for different platforms, tracking multiple dashboards, and managing support issues. It's rarely worth the time.

So, unless you've already maximized Amazon and are looking to scale further, my advice is simple: stick to what works. Focus on Amazon and double down.

3

WHAT DO YOU PUBLISH?

In the world of self-publishing, most books fall into one of four categories: no content, low-content, fiction, and nonfiction. Let's break each one down—starting with the simplest.

No Content

No-content books are exactly what they sound like—completely blank inside. No lines, no prompts, no images. Just empty pages. These books are designed to give the buyer full creative freedom, whether they want to sketch, write, or simply doodle.

Think of products like blank journals, notebooks, or sketchbooks. They're quick to produce since you don't need to write any content, but they rely heavily on niche targeting, smart cover design, and volume sales to succeed.

Low Content

Low-content books include minimal text but offer structured pages designed for interaction. They provide space for users to engage in specific activities like journaling, planning, coloring, or tracking information.

Examples of low-content books include guided journals, planners, logbooks, coloring books, puzzle books, and diaries. These types of books are quick to produce and don't require long-form writing, but success often depends on niche selection, presentation, and strong cover design.

Fiction

Fiction books are imaginative works that tell stories crafted from the author's creativity rather than real-life events. They transport readers into made-up worlds, characters, and plots, offering entertainment, emotion, and escape.

Fiction spans a wide range of genres—romance, mystery, fantasy, science fiction, thrillers, historical fiction, and more. These books can be powerful, memorable, and bestselling, but they typically require strong storytelling skills and consistent writing quality to succeed.

Nonfiction

Nonfiction books are grounded in reality. They're written to inform, educate, or explain real events, ideas, and concepts. Unlike fiction, these works are based on facts and research, not imagination.

Nonfiction covers a vast range of topics—history, biographies, self-help, science, technology, philosophy, politics, and more. These books often solve problems, answer questions, or share insights, making them especially appealing to readers looking for practical value or personal growth.

So, What Should I Publish?

I've experimented with all four types—no content, low content, fiction, and nonfiction. If you're looking for my honest recommendation, go with nonfiction.

Here's why:

No-content and low-content books are quick to create and a great way to get started. But they're *highly* competitive. You'll be up against thousands of similar products, many priced low (around $6.99), which means your royalty per sale is roughly $2. That doesn't leave much room for advertising. To make just $100, you'd need to sell 50 copies—compared to only 20 book sales earning $5 in royalties.

On top of that, this space is saturated with big players—companies with huge catalogs and deep pockets. They can afford to break even or even lose money upfront just to hook readers into their broader ecosystems. Competing with that is tough.

Also, low-content books don't translate well into eBooks or audiobooks, so you're missing out on extra income streams.

As for fiction, I gave it a shot too—using ghostwriters. Some books did okay, but relying on fiction writers is risky. If they leave, it's hard to find a replacement who can match their tone and style. Plus, fiction readers tend to prefer eBooks over paperbacks, which means lower royalties (around $2 per sale vs. $5+ for paperbacks). Keyword targeting is also more difficult, making it harder to run effective ads (we'll delve into keywords in the next chapter and amazon ads in chapter 20).

Nonfiction, on the other hand, checks all the boxes. It allows for higher pricing, better margins, and more straightforward keyword targeting. Just one well-positioned nonfiction book can consistently generate passive income—and that's scalable.

That said, not all nonfiction is created equal. I recommend avoiding categories like cookbooks and travel guides. They often require high-quality color images, which are expensive to source and result in higher printing costs—ultimately eating into your royalties.

So, if you're just getting started and want the best balance of speed, income potential, and scalability, nonfiction books (with black-and-white interiors) are your best bet.

4

KEYWORDS

Keywords are the backbone of your book's discoverability. Think of them as digital signposts, guiding shoppers through the vast marketplace of titles to find exactly what they want. Put simply, a keyword is whatever someone might search for when trying to find a book like yours. It's what your friend, parent, or grandparent would type in if they were looking for a particular topic or interest on Amazon.

Here are a few examples:

• Ketogenic diet for women

• Gardening in a small backyard

• Stretching for seniors

• Puppy training

• Kid-friendly riddles

A common mistake many new authors make is writing a book and then wondering why it isn't selling. The answer is often simple: they haven't chosen the right keywords. Even the best-written book will struggle to sell if readers can't find it.

That's why keyword research should come *before* you start writing. You want to make sure there's a proven audience actively searching for the topic you plan to publish. This approach not only boosts your chances of success but also helps you create books that people are actually looking for.

Niches, Subniches, and Book Topics

When searching for the right keywords, it's important to understand a few related terms that can help you categorize and target your content effectively. At the broadest level, you have a niche, which is essentially a general area of interest or category that can contain various subtopics. It's like an umbrella under which more specific themes reside. For example, "pet training" is a niche that covers a wide range of topics related to teaching animals new behaviors.

Within a niche, you'll find subniches, which are more focused segments of the broader category. These allow you to zoom in on specific aspects of the larger topic, making it easier to stand out and connect with a particular audience. If "pet training" is the niche, then "cat training" is a subniche within it.

Digging even deeper, you reach the book topic, which is the most specific level within a subniche. This is the exact subject your book will cover, often acting as a primary keyword for your marketing efforts. For example, "Clicker Training for Cats" might be a book topic within the "cat training" subniche, while "Gluten-Free Hand-Rolled Gnocchi with Vegan Sauces" could be a topic within the broader cooking niche.

To illustrate this hierarchy, consider the following examples. In the world of pets, you might have: books on animals as the broad category, books on pets as the subcategory, books on cats as the sub-subcategory, and eventually books on clicker training for shy or fearful Siamese cats as the highly specific book topic.

Similarly, in cooking, you could start with the broad category of cooking, narrow it down to international cuisine as the subcategory, then Italian cuisine as the sub-subcategory, and finally gluten-free hand-rolled gnocchi with vegan sauces as the precise book topic.

Understanding these levels can guide you in targeting your intended audience effectively and selecting the most relevant keywords. To start identifying potential niches, a simple way is to explore Amazon's main categories by searching "Amazon book best-sellers lists" on Google and clicking the first link.

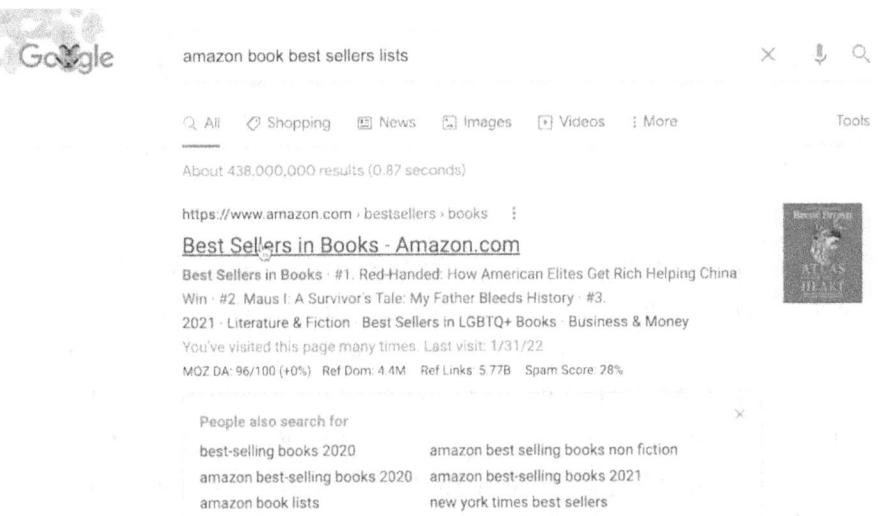

Once you're on the page, you'll see a list of categories on the left side. These cover a wide range of topics, including arts and photography, business and investing, education and reference, health, fitness, dieting, self-help, and many more. This is a great place to start when brainstorming potential niches for your book, as it gives you a sense of the major themes readers are interested in.

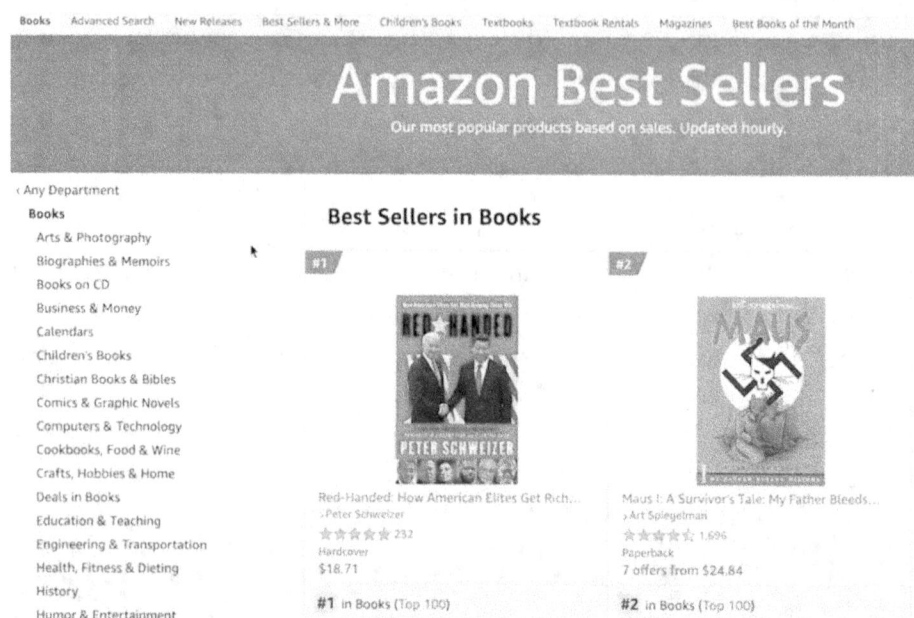

To narrow our focus, it's better to avoid targeting a broad main niche, as these categories tend to be too competitive and challenging to rank in. Instead, we should drill down into more specific layers. For example, if you choose the Crafts, Hobbies & Home category, you can click through to Crafts & Hobbies, and then refine further to something like Candlemaking. This approach helps you target a more defined audience, making it easier for your book to stand out and reach the right readers.

So, to summarize, we just clicked through:

Crafts, Hobbies & Home → Crafts & Hobbies → Candlemaking

(Niche) → (Sub-niche) → (Keyword)

As you explore potential book topics, you'll notice that many of the most promising ideas lie in specialized, less conventional niches. You might wonder if there's even a market for something as specific as **candlemaking** or **beekeeping for beginners**. Still, there's a well-known saying in business: *the riches are in the niches*. By focusing on these unique, targeted subjects, you're likely to encounter less competition, which makes it easier to stand out and rank on Amazon.

Here are some examples of keywords that fit this approach:

• Beekeeping for beginners

• Gut health

• Rental property investing

- Chess for kids
- Off-grid living
- Budgeting for college students
- Food truck business
- Meditation for entrepreneurs
- How to make small talk
- Public speaking for beginners
- Leadership for women
- Cognitive behavioral therapy
- Social media marketing
- How to read music
- At-home workouts
- Decluttering your home

Notice how many of these keywords focus on specific skills, challenges, or lifestyle choices. You can go even deeper into a niche by adding qualifiers like "for beginners," "for seniors," or "for women." For example:

- Ketogenic diet → Ketogenic diet for beginners
- Ketogenic diet → Ketogenic diet for seniors
- Ketogenic diet → Ketogenic diet for women over 50

Now, let's consider what **doesn't** qualify as a strong keyword. These might include overly broad terms or phrases that lack a clear, specific focus:

- Self-help
- Exercise
- Diet
- Music
- Outdoors
- Love
- Why anxiety sucks
- I can't lose weight
- Atomic habits
- Think and grow rich
- Money secrets
- Tony Robbins
- Money magic
- Weight loss magic for women
- Math

While some of these may sound appealing, they're too general to target effectively. Plus, using famous book titles or well-known personal brands can lead to issues with Amazon's guidelines, potentially resulting in your book being flagged or removed.

The goal is to find keywords that strike a balance between being specific enough to target a defined audience, yet broad enough to attract meaningful traffic. This sweet spot is where you'll find the most profitable book topics.

Keyword Profitability

To evaluate the profitability of a keyword, you need to understand the concept of Best Sellers Rank (BSR). This is a numerical value on Amazon that reflects how well a product is selling relative to others in its category, and it's updated hourly. The lower the BSR, the higher the sales volume.

For instance, a book with a BSR of 1 is the top-selling book across all of Amazon in its category, while a BSR of 100,000 indicates that it's the 100,000th best-selling book. While that might sound like a low ranking, books with a BSR under 100,000 are still selling consistently and are generally considered profitable targets for self-publishers.

It's also important to note that each book format—eBooks, paperbacks, and hardbacks—has its own separate BSR, so it's a good idea to check the rankings for each format when evaluating a keyword. This approach will give you a more accurate picture of a keyword's potential profitability.

To find the BSR of a book, simply scroll down to the Product Details section on its Amazon page, where you'll see all the relevant sales information.

```
Product details
    ASIN : B0875Z2J69
    Publisher : Independently published (April 14, 2020)
    Language : English
    Paperback : 132 pages
    ISBN-13 : 979-8637201709
    Item Weight : 7.8 ounces
    Dimensions : 6 x 0.33 x 9 inches
    Best Sellers Rank: #39,569 in Books (See Top 100 in Books)
        #1 in Candle Making (Books)
        #2 in Business of Art Reference
        #46 in Crafts & Hobbies Reference
    Customer Reviews: 4.6 ★★★★☆   697 ratings
```

Useful Tools

To speed up your keyword research, I recommend installing a free Chrome extension called **DS Amazon Quick View**. This plugin allows you to see the BSR of each book directly on the Amazon search results page, rather than having to click through to each individual product page.

To find it, just search "DS Amazon Quick View" on Google and click the first link.

Once installed, you'll see the BSR displayed beneath each book's title, giving you a quick overview of how well different keywords are performing.

KDSpy

Another powerful tool I recommend is KDSpy. Unlike DS Amazon Quick View, this one isn't free—it's a one-time payment of $69. But it's a worthwhile investment for serious self-publishers.

So, what exactly does KDSpy do? It's a Chrome extension that extracts critical book data from the first page of Amazon search results, presenting it in a clear, organized format. It gives you a comprehensive overview of a keyword's competition, average sales figures, estimated monthly revenue, and other key metrics, all at a glance.

Why is this important? While it's possible to manually gather this information by clicking through multiple pages and compiling data yourself, it's time-consuming and can be overwhelming. KDSpy cuts through that noise, saving you hours of research and giving you the insights you need to make profitable decisions quickly.

Like any business, investing a little upfront can significantly boost your long-term profits, and KDSpy is one of those smart investments that can pay off quickly. I've included a link at the back of this book if you decide to get it.

These two tools—DS Amazon Quick View and KDSpy—are all you really need to streamline your keyword research and gain a competitive edge.

Analyzing the Data

To see how KDSpy works in practice, let's walk through an example. Suppose you're evaluating the keyword "Candle making." After typing this into Amazon and activating the KDSpy Chrome extension, the tool will quickly pull data from all the books on the first page of search results, presenting it in a clear, organized table.

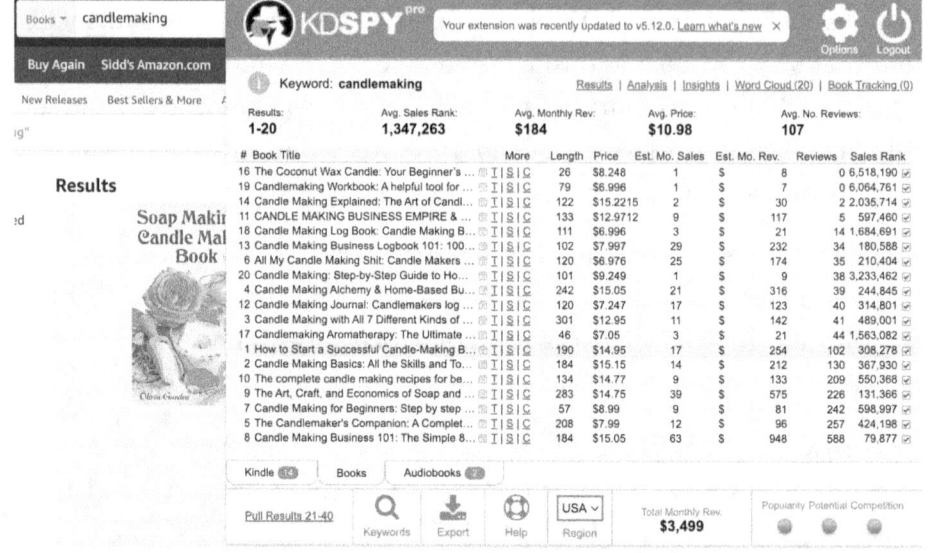

Two of the most important columns to pay attention to are "Estimated Monthly Revenue (Est. Mo. Rev.)" and "Reviews."

First, it's worth noting that the revenue figures shown in KDSpy don't reflect the author's actual profit. Instead, they represent the total earnings generated by Amazon. For example, if a book shows an estimated monthly revenue of $254, this means Amazon is earning that amount from the book, while the author typically takes home around a third of that, or roughly $84 after printing costs and Amazon's cut.

Next, pay close attention to the Reviews column. Our goal is to identify books with 100 reviews or less. Why this cutoff? Because if books with fewer than 100 reviews are generating decent revenue, it's a strong indicator that the niche isn't too competitive. This means that if you create a similar book and gather a modest number of reviews (around 15 to 30), you could potentially achieve similar success.

This strategy works because lower review counts usually mean the market isn't saturated, giving you a better shot at standing out and gaining traction. Fewer reviews also mean you won't need to overcome the social proof barrier as much, making it easier to break in and capture a share of the profits.

What to Look For

When evaluating a keyword like "Candlemaking" in KDSpy, it's important to focus on two main criteria: revenue potential and competition. Specifically, we're looking for books with fewer than 100 reviews that still generate a reasonable amount of monthly revenue.

In this example, the highest revenue for a book with under 100 reviews is $316, which translates to a rough author profit of around $105. Ideally, I like to see at least two or three other books within this range, as this indicates a healthier demand for the topic. If multiple low-review books are generating decent income, it's a strong sign that there's room for a new book to compete.

Unfortunately, in this case, the demand isn't quite there. While one book with 34 reviews earns $232 and another with 102 reviews makes $254, this still suggests a relatively limited market. Given the time and effort required to produce a high-quality book, these figures might not justify the investment.

As a general rule, I aim for keywords where at least two or three books with fewer than 100 reviews each generate at least $500 in monthly revenue. The more books that meet this criteria, the more confident I am that the keyword is worth pursuing. This approach increases the odds that your book will be profitable and less likely to struggle against established competitors.

Conclusion

To wrap up this stage of the keyword research process, it's crucial to ensure that the keyword you're considering actually appears in the titles of the books you're analyzing. This step helps you avoid misleading data and ensures you're targeting the right audience. You can do this by simply hovering over the book titles in KDSpy or on the Amazon search page to confirm that the exact keyword is present. If it is, that's a positive sign—you're on the right track.

It's also a good idea to perform your searches in an incognito window. This prevents your browsing history, personalized recommendations, and other stored data from influencing the results, giving you a more accurate view of the true market demand.

In summary, the main question to ask yourself at this stage is: Are there at least three books with fewer than 100 reviews, each making at least $500 in monthly revenue, and featuring your target keyword in their titles? If the answer is yes, you're likely looking at a promising keyword with solid profit potential. If not, it's probably best to keep searching, unless this is your very first book and you're more focused on learning the process than maximizing profit.

Choosing a keyword without sufficient demand or market interest can lead to a lot of wasted time and effort, so it's worth being thorough at this stage.

Chapter Summary

In this chapter, we covered the basics of understanding and identifying profitable keywords for your book. Keywords are the specific words or phrases that define and categorize a book's content, acting as digital signposts that guide potential readers to your title. They should reflect what a reader might type into the Amazon search bar, like "ketogenic diet for women" or "how to train a puppy."

To find the right keywords, it's essential to break down subjects from broad categories into more specific, targeted topics. For example, you might start with cooking as a broad category, narrow it down to international cuisine as a subcategory, then drill further into Italian cuisine before finally landing on a highly specific book topic like gluten-free hand-rolled gnocchi with vegan sauces. This approach helps you reach a more defined audience with less competition.

Avoid overly broad or non-specific terms like "self-help" or "diet," as these are often too competitive and lack the focus needed to stand out. Instead, explore Amazon's main niches by searching for "Amazon book best-sellers lists" and clicking through categories to find more refined ideas, like "candlemaking" or "off-grid living."

To streamline this process, consider using tools like DS Amazon Quick View and KDSpy. The former lets you quickly check a book's Best Sellers Rank (BSR) directly on the Amazon search page, while the latter extracts detailed sales data to help you assess competition and profitability. While KDSpy isn't free, it can save you significant time and offer valuable insights that might otherwise be challenging to gather manually.

When analyzing keyword profitability, aim for topics where at least three books have fewer than 100 reviews but are generating at least $500 in monthly revenue. Also, make sure your keyword appears in the book titles to ensure you're targeting the right market. For accurate results, use an incognito window when searching to avoid personalized biases from your browsing history.

In short, choose your keywords wisely. Not only do they help your book get discovered, but researching keywords can also spark ideas for what types of books to create in the first place. By identifying what readers are actively searching for, you can align your content with real demand—saving time, increasing your chances of success, and making smarter decisions from the very beginning.

5

ENROLLING IN KDP SELECT

KDP Select is a 90-day program designed exclusively for Kindle eBooks. By enrolling, you gain access to a broader audience through Amazon's Kindle Unlimited (KU) platform, which allows subscribers to read as many books as they want for a fixed monthly fee. This means your book can reach readers who might not have purchased it outright, potentially boosting your overall royalties through pages read.

However, there's a catch. To join KDP Select, you must make your eBook exclusive to Amazon for the full 90-day period. This means you can't sell or distribute the digital version of your book on any other platform or website during this time. While this restriction limits your distribution options, it also allows you to take full advantage of Amazon's promotional tools, like free and discounted book promotions, which can help drive more visibility and sales.

KDP Select Benefits

KDP Select comes with a few key benefits that can help you reach a larger audience and potentially boost your book's sales:

First, you earn royalties from the KDP Select Global Fund whenever someone reads your book through Kindle Unlimited (KU). This fund is a pool of money that Amazon sets aside each month to compensate authors based on the number of pages read. However, it's worth noting that these payouts are often modest—typically just a few extra dollars per month unless your book is particularly popular within the KU program.

Second, you gain access to Kindle Countdown Deals. This feature allows you to temporarily discount your eBook and create a sense of urgency with a visible countdown timer. For example, you could drop the price of a $6.99 book to $0.99 for one day, then gradually increase it to $1.99, $2.99, and so on over the course of a few days. You can run these promotions for a total of five days within each 90-day enrollment period. This can be a great way to spike sales and visibility without permanently reducing your book's list price.

Third, you have the option to use the Free Book Promotion tool. This allows you to make your book free for up to five days within each 90-day cycle. Unlike Kindle Countdown Deals, this isn't just for KU readers—your book is free to anyone visiting Amazon. You can choose to run these five days consecutively or spread them out over several smaller campaigns. For example, you might run a two-day free promo in the first month, then follow up with a three-day free promo a month later.

I personally like this approach, as it can help you capture a larger pool of readers and potentially gain more reviews. When a reader downloads your book during a free promotion and leaves a review, that review is marked as "verified," which carries more weight than an unverified review. This verified status can make a big difference, as social proof is a decisive factor in convincing new readers to take a chance on your book.

(Unverified review)

(Verified review)

Should I Join KDP Select?

In my opinion, yes. While I can't provide concrete evidence, I genuinely believe that Amazon tends to promote books enrolled in KDP Select more than those that aren't. It makes sense from a business perspective—if Amazon stands to earn more from books in the program, they're likely to push them more in search results, recommendations, and promotional emails.

I've also tried the alternative route, removing my books from KDP Select to go "wide" by uploading them to platforms like Draft2Digital, which distributes to sites like Apple Books, Kobo, Barnes & Noble, and others. But the results were underwhelming. Despite having over fifty eBooks available, I was only making around $100 to $200 per month at most across all those platforms combined. The extra effort simply didn't justify the modest returns.

This is a good example of the 80/20 rule in action—80% of your results often come from 20% of your efforts. In this case, focusing on Amazon's platform through **KDP Select** can significantly streamline your business and maximize your earnings.

6

PEN NAMES

When it comes to publishing on Amazon KDP, one of the first branding decisions you'll face is choosing the name that appears on your book. You have three main options: your real name, a pen name, or a brand name. Each one comes with its own set of benefits and trade-offs, and the right choice depends on your goals, niche, and personal comfort level.

Real Name

Using your real name is the most direct and transparent option. It's ideal if you're building a personal brand—especially in niches like self-help, finance, or memoir—where readers often want to know the person behind the ideas. It also allows for more personal interaction: book signings, interviews, podcast appearances, and public recognition all become easier when you're not hiding behind a pseudonym. The downside? If you later switch topics or want to separate your identity from your books, it becomes harder to pivot without confusing your audience.

Pen Names

Pen names offer a great deal of creative freedom, privacy, and flexibility—especially if you're writing in multiple genres or want to keep your publishing work separate from your day job or personal life. Maybe you're writing steamy romance novels but work in corporate law, or perhaps you're exploring sensitive or controversial topics and prefer to maintain a degree of separation from your real identity. Sometimes, a pen name simply fits the tone of a genre better than your real name would. Whatever the reason, the key to using a pen name effectively is consistency: once you choose a name, stick with it for that niche and treat it as a legitimate author brand.

There are many reasons why authors choose to use pen names. For some, it's about maintaining privacy or anonymity. Others want to create a clear divide between their professional and writing lives. A pen name can also be a strategic choice—helping align the tone and personality of the name with the expectations of a particular genre or avoiding potential bias that might come with a real name. It also allows authors to build distinct identities for each niche they write in—using a playful name for children's books and a more authoritative one for financial guides, for instance.

I've personally created separate pen names for different niches, such as language learning and history, to keep my brands distinct and avoid confusing readers. It's the same strategy used by many successful authors. Take Stephen King, for example—he's closely associated with horror. If he suddenly released a historical romance or a gardening guide under the same name, it would likely throw off his audience. That's why even bestselling authors sometimes use different names for different genres. J.K. Rowling did exactly this when she published *The Cuckoo's Calling* under the pen name Robert Galbraith, to distinguish her detective novels from the world of *Harry Potter*.

Managing multiple pen names on Amazon is actually pretty straightforward. You can publish under different names all within a single KDP account—there's no need to create separate logins. Just make sure to avoid using the name of a famous person (like "Stephen King"), as that violates Amazon's guidelines. Also, if you plan to use professional titles like "Dr." or "PhD" in your pen name, Amazon may ask for proof to verify authenticity.

Having different pen names allows me to separate niches—like language learning and history—without confusing readers. Each pen name becomes its own little brand, complete with its own style, tone, and even email list. This means when I release a new book in that niche, I can contact readers who already enjoyed my past books, increasing my chances of repeat sales and early reviews. I'll talk more about building an email list in chapter 20, but just know that pen names can make this process much easier.

That said, you don't need to overthink your name. Spend five or ten minutes, pick something that feels like a good fit for your niche, and move forward. If you're stuck, try a pen name generator like Reedsy's free tool—it can help spark some ideas.

And while pen names work great for authors who want to write across multiple genres or maintain privacy, some choose to go a different route entirely—publishing under a brand name instead.

Brand

Some authors, particularly those publishing low-content books like journals, planners, and coloring books, or those managing a team of ghostwriters, choose to publish under a brand name rather than a personal or pen name. These brand names—such as "Mindful Press" or "BrightPath Learning"—give off a polished, professional impression that can lend authority to your books and make your publishing operation feel more like a business. A well-chosen brand name can also serve as an umbrella for multiple genres, series, or pen names, allowing for scalability as you grow your catalog.

This works especially well in niches such as education, wellness, activity books, or workbooks for kids—areas where readers often care more about the usefulness of the product than the individual behind it. However, it's important to understand the tradeoff: brand names tend to lack the personal connection that readers seek in genres like memoir, fiction, or self-help. In those cases, using a real or pen name might better foster trust and emotional resonance. Ultimately, a brand name works best when you want the product itself to shine more than the personality behind it.

Due Diligence

Whichever naming route you choose—real, pen, or brand—make sure to do a little due diligence before locking it in. First, search Amazon to ensure the name isn't already being used by another author. Then run a quick Google search to make sure it's not associated with anything controversial or problematic—you'd be surprised what can turn up. It's also smart to check the meaning of your chosen name in other languages using Google Translate or ChatGPT, especially if you plan to sell internationally. And if you're going with a brand name, take one final step and run a trademark search at uspto.gov/trademarks/search to confirm it's legally available. A few minutes of research now can save you a major headache later.

7

BOOK IDEATION & OUTLINES

When starting out, it's important to set realistic expectations for your first book. It's unlikely to generate significant earnings right away, and there's even a chance it might not make any money at all. This is perfectly normal, and it shouldn't discourage you. Instead of aiming for perfection, view your first book as a learning experience—a stepping stone to building the skills you need for long-term success. The faster you finish it and move on to your second or third book, the sooner you'll see real results.

Now, let's talk about choosing a topic. My first book was about growing and selling Instagram accounts, a subject I knew well after spending a year in the field. I recommend following a similar approach—pick a topic you're knowledgeable about. This could be a hobby, like playing a musical instrument or a sport you enjoy, or it could be something related to your profession. You might even consider writing about your city, sharing interesting facts and insights, or exploring a unique aspect of your culture or background if you come from a different country. The key is to choose a topic you genuinely care about, as this will make the writing process more enjoyable and engaging.

To give you some inspiration, here are a few book ideas I've seen on Amazon that have done well:

1. Raised bed gardening

2. Stretching for seniors

3. The New York travel guide (you can replace New York with your city)

4. Personal finance for teens

5. 101 creative side hustles

6. Easy vegan recipes for beginners

7. Keto diet recipes

8. Growing fruit trees

9. Overcoming self-doubt and imposter syndrome

10. The freelancer's survival guide

11. How to build a tiny house

12. Gut health for women

I hope these examples spark some ideas and help you identify a topic for your first book. Remember, the goal is to choose something you're passionate about and knowledgeable in, as this will make the writing process much smoother and more enjoyable.

Structuring Your Book

Creating a well-organized outline is an essential first step in the writing process. Think of your outline as the roadmap for your book, similar to a table of contents. It gives your writing direction and ensures you cover all the important points without losing focus.

There's no one-size-fits-all approach to outlining. Some books work best with a few long, in-depth chapters, while others benefit from a series of shorter, more focused sections. For example, when I wrote my Instagram Mastery book, I based the structure on the most common questions I received about growing and monetizing Instagram accounts. Here's a rough version of that outline:

1. Starting with the End in Mind
2. Niche Selection
3. Selecting a Username
4. Ideal Profile Picture
5. Adding Analytics
6. Optimizing Your Bio
7. Adding Links the Right Way
8. Getting Started
9. What to Post
10. How to Find Accounts
11. Creating Photos
12. The Perfect Video
13. All About Stories
14. When to Post
15. Ideal Image Sizes
16. Feed Consistency
17. The Perfect Caption
18. What Hashtags to Use
19. Analyzing Accounts
20. Growing Your Account
21. Bots and Software
22. Becoming Personal
23. How to Contact Accounts
24. How to Monetize Your Account
25. How to Do Ads on Other Accounts
26. Bonus Niches

This approach worked well because each chapter addressed a specific question or topic, making the book practical and easy to navigate. You can use a similar method by breaking your topic into common questions or areas of interest.

Alternatively, you might organize your outline around a step-by-step guide, a chronological progression, or even a series of case studies, depending on the nature of your book. Here are some other ways of coming up with book outlines:

Mind Mapping

Start with a central idea or theme and branch out into subtopics or chapters.

Central idea: Personal Development

- Branches:

- Goal Setting
- Building Self-Confidence
- Time Management
- Overcoming Fear and Anxiety
- Developing Positive Habits
- Finding Life Purpose

Chronological Order

If your book covers a series of events, a historical progression, or a personal journey, it makes sense to structure it in chronological order. This approach works well for biographies, memoirs, historical accounts, or any book that benefits from a clear beginning, middle, and end. It allows readers to follow the narrative naturally as it unfolds over time.

Book: The Evolution of Space Exploration

Chapter 1: Early Astronomical Discoveries

Chapter 2: The Space Race (1950s-1970s)

Chapter 3: The Shuttle Era (1980s-2000s)

Chapter 4: The Rise of Private Spaceflight (2000s-Present)

Chapter 5: The Future of Space Travel

Problem-Solution

If your book is focused on solving specific problems or addressing common challenges, it makes sense to organize it by problem and solution. This approach breaks the content into clear sections, each dedicated to a particular issue and the steps needed to overcome it.

Book: Managing Anxiety

- Section 1: Understanding Anxiety

- Chapter 1: What Causes Anxiety?
- Chapter 2: Recognizing Anxiety Triggers

- Section 2: Coping Strategies for Anxiety

- Chapter 3: Mindfulness and Relaxation Techniques
- Chapter 4: Building a Support Network

Comparative Analysis

If your book aims to highlight the differences and similarities between various concepts, ideas, or approaches, a comparative structure can be highly effective. This format allows you to explore each topic in depth while providing a clear framework for readers to follow.

Book: Leadership Styles in Business

- Chapter 1: Introduction to Leadership Theories
- Chapter 2: Authoritative vs. Democratic Leadership
- Chapter 3: Transformational vs. Transactional Leadership
- Chapter 4: Servant Leadership vs. Charismatic Leadership
- Chapter 5: Choosing the Right Leadership Style for Your Team

Topical Organization

If your book covers a broad subject with multiple areas of focus, it makes sense to organize it by major themes or topics. This approach breaks your content into clearly defined sections, each of which can contain several chapters dedicated to specific aspects of the broader topic.

Book: The Complete Fitness Guide

- Section 1: Building Physical Strength

  - Chapter 1: Strength Training Fundamentals
  - Chapter 2: Effective Bodyweight Exercises

- Section 2: Improving Flexibility and Mobility

  - Chapter 3: Stretching Techniques for Beginners

- Chapter 4: Advanced Mobility Drills

- Section 3: Mental Health and Well-being

- Chapter 5: The Importance of Recovery
- Chapter 6: Building Mental Resilience

Keep in mind that these are just a few approaches to outlining, and you can always mix and match them to fit your book's specific needs. The goal is to create a clear, organized structure that keeps you focused during the writing process and ensures your final book is cohesive, engaging, and easy for readers to follow.

8

GETTING STARTED WITH YOUR FIRST BOOK

Choosing the right topic for your first book is one of the most important early decisions you'll make. Ideally, you'll find something that not only excites you but also has a solid keyword or demand behind it (so you can make some sales on Amazon). But even if your first book doesn't hit a high-traffic keyword, don't worry. Think of this first project less as a bestseller and more as your training ground. This is where you learn the ropes, build confidence, and refine your process so that every book you write afterward comes together with more clarity and precision.

My approach to early books was exactly that—practice and momentum. I set a simple goal: write 10,000 words in ten days, aiming for about 1,000 focused words per day. I didn't obsess over perfection. Instead, I focused on showing up, writing with intention, and building discipline. The faster you complete your first draft, the quicker you'll learn what works, what doesn't, and what feels natural for your voice and workflow. Each book teaches you something. The second will be smoother than the first, and the fifth smoother still. Writing becomes less daunting and more second nature.

When I first started out, I wrote nine 10,000-word books across three niches. I didn't know which would be profitable—I was testing. One of those niches eventually took off, so I doubled down on it. What's amazing is that several of those early books still sell to this day. That's the beauty of this model: once your book is up, it can continue generating passive income long after you've moved on to new projects.

But I want to be clear about something: even though I advocate for speed and consistency, I don't believe in publishing junk. I'm not here to push the idea that quantity should always trump quality. In fact, I believe in the opposite—writing things of substance that come from genuine knowledge and lived experience. I may not be the best technical writer out there, but I know my topics inside and out. That's what gives the writing value. I've written about learning French because I spent years learning the language. I've written about history and quirky American facts because they've long been personal interests of mine. When you know your subject well, the depth comes through naturally.

Once I've picked a topic, I go deep. I start by identifying the top three bestselling books in that niche and read them cover to cover to understand what's already being said—and more importantly, what's being left out. But I don't stop there. I spend time combing through the reviews, especially the negative ones. These reviews are goldmines of insight. If readers complain that a book was too vague, lacked examples, or skipped key steps, I take note. These gaps become my opportunities. I use those comments as a blueprint for how to make my own book better—filling in the blanks, solving the pain points, and delivering what readers were hoping for the first time around.

At the same time, I tune in to my own learning process. As I research, I pay close attention to the thoughts and questions that come up for me. What confused me? What felt too glossed over? What did I wish someone had explained more clearly? These aren't just casual curiosities—they're clues to what readers might also struggle with. So I make a point of addressing those issues directly in my writing. Some of the most useful parts of my books come from answering the very questions I had at the start. It's a way to write not just as a teacher, but as someone who remembers what it's like to be new.

To round out my research, I watch YouTube videos, join niche Facebook groups, and lurk in Reddit threads. I pay close attention to how people talk about the topic—what questions they ask, what frustrations they share, what tips they give each other. This gives me a real sense of the language, mindset, and lived experience of the audience I'm writing for. By the time I sit down to write, I've absorbed so much context that the material flows more naturally. I'm no longer just collecting and repeating facts—I'm organizing them, adding clarity, and offering real-world insight. It's the difference between information and understanding.

This research-first approach has become a cornerstone of my writing process. I don't believe in pumping out books on topics I barely know just to fill a shelf. Whether it's French learning, history, or American facts—topics I was deeply passionate about from the start—or something entirely new, I take the time to become knowledgeable before I ever write a word. I want each book to feel like it was written by someone who knows what they're talking about. And by the time I'm done preparing, I genuinely do.

That said, there are times when I stumble across a keyword that's clearly profitable—low competition, high demand—but I just don't have the personal interest or expertise to do the topic justice. In those cases, I don't force it. Instead, I'll hire a ghostwriter who *is* passionate about the topic and knows it well. I give them a solid brief, based on my keyword research and an outline shaped by what's missing in the market. This way, the book still gets created with care and competence—even if I'm not the one writing every word. It's all about playing to your strengths, staying focused on quality, and making sure the end product delivers genuine value to the reader.

My process reflects this. I used to head to the same café each morning, order a strong black coffee, and throw on some classical music. I'd open a blank Google Doc, set a timer for 90 minutes, and commit to pure focus. No emails, no tabs, no scrolling. My only rule: write or sit in silence. Most days, I hit my goal of 1,000 words. Even if you only have 30 minutes a day, that's enough. What matters most is building the habit. Momentum compounds.

Once I had a draft, I wouldn't rush to publish. I'd take a break, then come back and read it with fresh eyes. That's when I'd notice the clutter, the awkward phrasing, and the moments that needed more punch. I'd revise slowly, section by section, improving the flow and tightening the structure. Only after completing that pass would I run the text through Grammarly to clean up any grammar or spelling issues. These days, I'll often drop paragraphs into ChatGPT and ask, "How can I say this more clearly?" or "Does this feel flat?" AI won't replace your voice, but it's an excellent tool to refine and enhance your writing if used wisely.

If typing feels like a chore, voice-to-text is a great option. Tools like Google Docs' voice typing or apps like Otter.ai can transcribe your thoughts while you're walking, driving, or cooking. Several authors I know use this method to free up their creativity and get past the blank-page anxiety.

At the end of the day, what matters is writing with care, not writing for speed alone. Your book doesn't have to be perfect—but it should reflect genuine effort, useful insight, and a desire to help or entertain your reader. If you start with a topic you care about, give yourself the space to write thoughtfully, and commit to improving draft by draft, your writing will resonate—even if you're not a "natural" writer. That's the kind of quality that matters, and it's what will set you apart in a marketplace flooded with fast but forgettable books.

9

IMAGES AND ILLUSTRATIONS

Including images and illustrations in your book isn't just about aesthetics—it's about engagement, comprehension, and memorability. Studies suggest that around 75% of all information processed by the brain is visual. This makes visual content an incredibly powerful tool for reinforcing key concepts, setting the tone, and making your book more enjoyable to read. Whether you're writing nonfiction, how-to guides, children's books, or even fiction with detailed world-building, the right image in the right place can go a long way.

Why Use Images?

Visuals serve multiple purposes in a book. They can break up dense text, give the reader a moment to pause, and improve overall readability. A compelling image can reinforce an idea in a way that text alone often can't. For example, a diagram can help clarify a complex process in a step-by-step guide, or an infographic can summarize data-heavy information into something more digestible. Photographs or illustrations can also establish the mood and give your book a unique identity.

Types of Visual Content to Include

- **Your Own Photos:** If you're handy with a camera and have access to high-resolution images, your own photography can add a personal, authentic touch to your book. This is especially effective in memoirs, travel guides, or instructional content where your own experience plays a central role.

- **Stock Images:** For broader visual needs, stock photo libraries offer a wide range of high-quality options. Paid sources like Adobe Stock, Shutterstock, Depositphotos, and iStock are great for professional-grade images. If you're on a tighter budget, check out free sites like Unsplash, Pexels, or Pixabay—but be sure to read the licensing terms carefully, as some images may require attribution or restrict commercial use.

- **Illustrations:** Custom illustrations are a fantastic way to add character and charm to your book, especially if you're working in genres like children's literature, creative nonfiction, self-help, or even educational content. An illustration at the start of each chapter or a handful of visuals scattered throughout the book can elevate the reader's experience and make your content more engaging.

If you're printing in black and white to save on production costs (which is recommended unless color images are essential), consider commissioning what's known as line art. These are black-and-white drawings—often simple, clean, and stylized—that reproduce beautifully in grayscale and avoid the muddy or low-quality appearance that some color images suffer when automatically converted to black and white during printing.

Hiring illustrators to create line art is surprisingly affordable. On platforms like Fiverr, Upwork, or even 99designs, you can find talented artists who offer hand-drawn or digital black-and-white illustrations for as little as $2–$10 per image, depending on complexity. This is a budget-friendly way to add a touch of uniqueness to your book without sacrificing quality.

When working with illustrators, be clear about your vision, page dimensions, and whether you need vector files or high-resolution PNGs. Most artists are happy to accommodate specific formatting if you mention it's for print or Kindle publication. And of course, always make sure you're purchasing the commercial rights to use and sell the illustrations in your book.

• **Diagrams, Flowcharts & Infographics:** Visual aids like diagrams, flowcharts, and infographics are powerful tools for simplifying complex information. They work especially well in nonfiction or educational books, where step-by-step processes, comparisons, or statistics can otherwise feel overwhelming. A clean diagram can explain a workflow in seconds. A well-crafted infographic can turn dense text into something instantly understandable and engaging.

If you're creating these visuals yourself, there are plenty of free tools that make the process easy. For diagrams and flowcharts, try draw.io, FigJam, or Excalidraw—each offers simple interfaces to map out systems or structures. For more polished infographics, Canva, Piktochart, and Venngage offer pre-designed templates that you can customize by dragging in charts, icons, and text blocks.

To speed things up, you can even use ChatGPT to help plan or generate the content for your visuals. Ask it to summarize key ideas, outline comparisons, or convert a block of text into bullet points for a chart. For example, you could prompt: "Summarize the top five reasons to self-publish versus traditionally publish in a format suitable for an infographic," and use the result as your foundation.

These visuals not only help readers retain information but also improve the pacing and visual rhythm of your book—making it feel more dynamic and reader-friendly.

• **AI-Generated Images:** Artificial intelligence has opened up new creative possibilities for authors. Tools like DALL·E, Midjourney, and ChatGPT allow you to generate completely custom visuals based on your *prompts*—short text descriptions that tell the AI what to create. For example, you might enter something like *a futuristic city at sunset in watercolor style* and the AI will generate an image that matches that request. The clearer and more specific your prompt, the better the results. This makes AI tools incredibly useful for producing unique artwork, illustrations, or concept visuals that might be hard to find through traditional stock image sites.

You can even use these AI tools to create illustrations, diagrams, or abstract visuals to set the mood for different sections of your book. However, there are two important caveats. First, AI-generated images don't always come out perfect—hands, text, and fine details can be inconsistent—so expect to experiment and refine your prompts. Second, Amazon now requires authors to disclose if any AI-generated content has been used in their book, including images. While this doesn't disqualify your book from being published, it's something to be aware of and transparent about when uploading your files.

Design and Formatting Tips

When designing and formatting your book, it's important to use high-quality images that enhance the reading experience without causing technical issues. For print books, make sure all images are at least 300 DPI (dots per inch). While lower-resolution images might look fine on screens, they can appear blurry or pixelated when printed. To ensure smooth uploading and optimal display, flatten all image layers before inserting them into your manuscript, and make sure each image is placed at 100% of its intended size. Oversized files can cause delays or errors during the publishing process, so it's best to resize them appropriately beforehand. Visually, your images should support the surrounding text—not overwhelm it. A well-placed visual can add clarity or break up dense content, but if it dominates the page or distracts from your message, it might do more harm than good. Aim for a balance between readability and visual appeal.

Choosing Between Color and Black & White

If you're self-publishing a print book through Amazon KDP, printing in color significantly increases your production costs. A smart workaround is to include color images in your ebook while printing in black and white for the paperback version. You can upload the same interior file and simply select "black and white" during the KDP print setup. Only opt for full-color printing if it's essential to your book's purpose (e.g., photography, design portfolios, or educational visuals that rely on color coding).

Legal Considerations

When using images in your book, it's crucial to ensure you have the legal right to include them. Many stock photo sites operate under Creative Commons licenses, which typically allow free use, but some images may require attribution or come with restrictions on commercial use. Always read the licensing terms carefully. Additionally, it's a good idea to run a quick Google search on any image, illustration, or character name you plan to include. This helps you avoid accidentally using content that's copyrighted, trademarked, or associated with something controversial. Taking a few extra minutes to verify image rights can save you from potential legal trouble later on.

Final Thoughts

Images can elevate your book from good to great. They improve readability, increase retention, and add visual flair—especially in genres like children's books, how-to guides, or anything involving step-by-step instructions. However, they're not strictly necessary for every project. If you're writing a nonfiction book that primarily delivers information—like a guide, a language course, or a topic-based explainer—then high-quality text alone can do the job just fine. Many bestselling nonfiction titles succeed without a single visual, relying instead on clarity, structure, and value-packed content. That said, when used intentionally, visuals can enhance the reader's experience and support your message in meaningful ways. Start small if you're new to this, and as your publishing skills and budget grow, so can your use of professional-grade visuals. The key is to make them work for your content—not just as decoration, but to truly add something valuable to the page.

10

POLISHING YOUR MANUSCRIPT

Congratulations on finishing the first 10,000 words (or more) of your book! That's no small feat, and it's a milestone worth celebrating. But as satisfying as it is to type "The End," this is where the real magic happens—because writing a book isn't just about what you put on the page. It's about what you revise, refine, and polish after the first draft is done.

Editing is the phase where your raw ideas get sharpened into something professional and enjoyable to read. It goes well beyond fixing grammar or cleaning up typos. It's about tightening structure, improving flow, enhancing clarity, and making sure the book delivers on the promise you set up in your title, subtitle, and opening pages.

Even if you followed an outline, it's common to discover that some chapters might need to be reordered, expanded, or even removed entirely. Sometimes you'll realize you went off on a tangent that slows the book down—or that a brief anecdote deserves to become a whole chapter of its own. Editing is the time to ask questions like: *Is this easy to follow? Is there a better way to explain this idea? Would a reader get stuck here?*

One of the most useful things I do during this phase is reading the manuscript out loud. This sounds simple, but it works. When you hear your words spoken, awkward phrasing, run-on sentences, and unclear explanations jump out in a way they often don't when you're just skimming silently. If you're not keen on reading it aloud yourself, there are free text-to-speech tools online that can do it for you. Listening to your work with fresh ears helps you spot things you would otherwise miss.

I usually do my first pass using the "Suggesting" mode in Google Docs. It's a fast way to catch easy wins—like wordy sentences, repeated phrases, or minor grammar issues. After that, I bring in Grammarly for a more technical review. It's not perfect, but it catches advanced grammar errors, passive voice, tone issues, and even awkward transitions. Think of it as a second set of eyes to help you polish things before involving anyone else.

But even with these tools, there's no substitute for human input. A good proofreader or editor will see your book from a reader's perspective and offer suggestions you'd never think of. They're not emotionally attached to your favorite paragraph or sentence. They'll tell you if something is confusing, redundant, or unnecessary. In my experience, this feedback is incredibly valuable.

If you hire an editor, expect at least one round of back and forth. You might get questions like *Can you clarify this point?* or suggestions like *Consider moving this to the introduction.* This process can feel uncomfortable at first—especially if you've put a lot of effort into your draft—but it's essential for growth. Editors don't just clean up your book. They challenge it, refine it, and help you produce something that stands out.

You don't need to spend thousands of dollars on editing—especially early on. Start by asking a friend to read the book and give honest feedback. If they get bored in chapter three or confused by chapter six, pay attention. Once you've done as much as you can on your own, a freelance editor from Fiverr or Upwork can often do a great job for $50–

$200, depending on the length of your book and the level of editing needed.

At this stage, your goal is simple: make the book as clear, clean, and reader-friendly as possible. You don't need to be a perfectionist. But you do want to put your best foot forward. A little extra polish here goes a long way—because once your book is live, it's out there for the world to see.

If you're feeling exhausted with your draft, that's normal. But remember: editing is where good books become great ones. Don't rush it. You've already done the hard part by getting the words on the page. Now it's time to make sure they shine.

11

FORMATTING YOUR BOOK

Formatting your book might not be the most glamorous part of the publishing process, but it's absolutely essential. A clean, professional layout makes your book easier to read and navigate, and far more appealing to potential buyers. If your text looks sloppy, cramped, or inconsistent, it can quickly turn readers away—even if the content itself is excellent.

Choosing the right font and style for your book is a crucial part of the formatting process. To ensure your book looks clean and professional on Kindle devices, it's best to stick with simple, widely supported fonts like Calibri or Arial for the main text. These fonts are reliable, easy to read, and less likely to cause formatting issues when your book is uploaded to Amazon.

If you're using Google Docs to write and format your manuscript, it's important to use the built-in Styles feature rather than manually changing fonts and sizes.

For chapter titles, use Heading 1. This is the largest default heading style in Google Docs and signals that the text is a top-level section, like a new chapter. It typically appears bold and significantly larger than the body text. This isn't just about how it looks—it also helps you generate a clean, clickable Table of Contents and makes things easier when converting your file for Kindle or print.

For subheadings within a chapter, use Heading 2 or Subtitle. These are smaller than Heading 1 but still stand out from the main text, helping to break up long chapters and improve readability.

When it comes to paragraph spacing, I recommend using the Open setting in Google Docs. It provides comfortable breathing room between lines without stretching the content too far apart. Stick with a font size between 10 and 12 points, which keeps the text highly readable while maximizing space. White space is another important factor—it prevents visual fatigue and gives the eye a place to rest. Long walls of text can be overwhelming, so breaking them up with spacing, bold text for emphasis, *italics* for tone, and bullet points where needed can make your book feel smoother and more enjoyable to read.

Even if you're using other formatting softwares these principles still apply. Most tools follow a similar hierarchy—Heading 1 for chapters, Heading 2 or similar for sub-sections, and Normal Text for the main content.

Inserting Page Breaks for a Professional Layout

Adding page breaks is a critical step in formatting your manuscript for Kindle and paperback. It ensures each chapter starts on a new page, giving your book a polished, professional look similar to a traditional print book. To insert a page break, simply place your cursor at the end of the text you want to separate and press Ctrl + Enter (or Command + Return on a Mac). This moves the following text to a new page, creating a clean division between sections.

If you accidentally add a page break or need to adjust one, just place your cursor at the beginning of the text on the new page and press Backspace to remove it.

Most authors usually add page breaks in the following places:

• After the Title and Author page

• After the Copyright page

• Before the Table of Contents

• Before the Conclusion

• Before the About the Author section

• Before the final Call to Action page, where I invite readers to leave a review

If you're unsure about where to place page breaks, it can be helpful to refer to a physical book for guidance. Many authors also prefer to start each chapter on a new page, even if it leaves some white space at the end of the previous chapter. This approach gives your book a more polished feel and makes it easier for readers to navigate.

Choosing the Right Book Size

Selecting the right dimensions for your book is an important part of the formatting process. For most nonfiction titles, the two most common sizes are 5x8 inches and 6x9 inches.

If your manuscript is on the shorter side, typically under 15,000 words, a 5x8 format can work well. On the other hand, if your book is closer to 20,000 words or more, the 6x9 size might be a better fit, providing a more substantial, professional look that's common for longer nonfiction titles.

As you dive deeper into formatting, you'll come across terms like page margins and bleed. These are more advanced concepts that control how your pages are laid out for printing, but they're not essential to master if you plan to hire a professional for this part of the process.

If you prefer to handle the formatting yourself, there are a few excellent tools available. Vellum is a popular choice for Mac users, known for its intuitive interface and professional-looking results. It also includes various tutorial videos to guide you through the process. For PC users, Atticus is a great alternative, offering similar functionality and a user-friendly design. Both tools can save you a lot of time and effort, making the formatting stage much easier.

12

SETTING UP YOUR KDP ACCOUNT

KDP, which stands for Kindle Direct Publishing, started as a platform for eBooks but has since expanded to include paperbacks and hardcovers. Despite this growth, the platform has kept its original name.

Before you can upload your book, you'll need to create a KDP account. Keep in mind that Amazon's terms and conditions only allow one KDP account per person. Attempting to create multiple accounts can lead to all of them being permanently suspended, so it's important to stick to a single account.

You have two options for signing up: you can either use your existing Amazon shopping account or create a brand new account with a different email address. To get started, go to kdp.amazon.com/signin and click the yellow "Get Started" button in the top right corner.

The sign-up process can be a bit time-consuming, as you'll need to provide important details, including your Social Security number for tax purposes and your bank account routing numbers for direct deposit payments. These steps are essential to ensure you receive your royalties smoothly each month.

Once your account is set up, you'll be taken to the KDP dashboard, where you'll see four main tabs: Bookshelf, Reports, Community, and Marketing. This is where you'll manage your books, track sales, and access promotional tools.

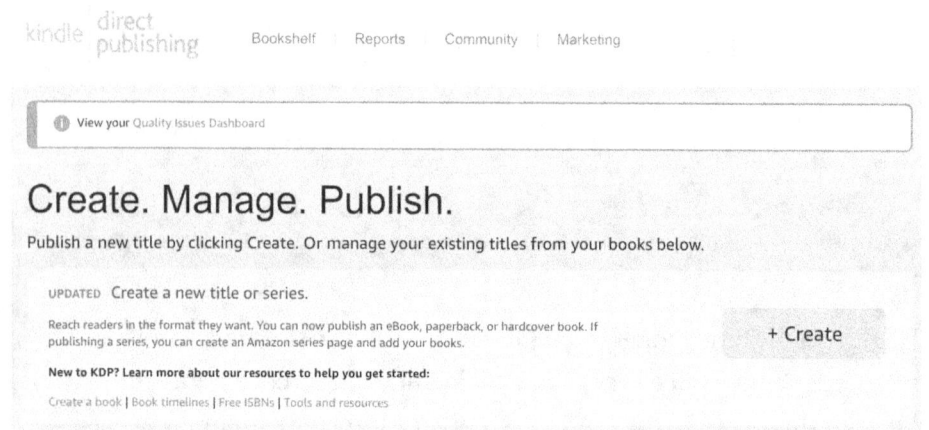

Understanding the Bookshelf

The Bookshelf is where you'll upload all your new books and manage your existing titles. To add a new book, simply click the large yellow "+ Create" button. You'll then be presented with a few options, including Kindle eBook, Paperback, Hardcover, and Series.

The Series option is useful if you're planning to publish multiple books within the same series, as it helps link the titles together, making it easier for readers to find related books and continue their reading journey.

For the purposes of this guide, we'll be focusing on the two main formats —Kindle eBook and Paperback—which we'll cover in more detail in chapters 14 and 15.

Reports

The Reports section of your KDP account is where you'll keep an eye on your earnings. In late 2022, Amazon updated this section, adding a range of useful tabs, including Dashboard, Orders, KENP Read (Kindle Edition Normalized Pages Read), Month-to-Date, Promotions, Pre-orders, and Royalties Estimator.

The KENP Read tab is particularly important if you have books enrolled in Kindle Select, as it tracks the total number of pages read by Kindle Unlimited subscribers. This data directly impacts your earnings from the KDP Select Global Fund.

For Kindle eBooks, Amazon offers two royalty rates: 35% and 70%. The 35% rate applies globally, while the 70% rate is available in select territories, including the United States, the United Kingdom, Australia, and several other countries. However, this higher rate comes with a few conditions, such as minimum and maximum pricing requirements, and can be influenced by factors like VAT, promotional pricing, and delivery costs.

For paperback books, Amazon keeps 40% and pays you the remaining 60% after deducting printing costs. Unlike eBook royalties, which are calculated immediately, paperback royalties are distributed two months after the month in which they were earned. To receive a payment, your royalties must reach a minimum balance of $100, and payments are typically made via direct deposit on the last day of the month. The exact timing may vary depending on your bank and location.

While the delay in receiving your first payments can be a bit frustrating, the long-term potential for passive income makes the wait worthwhile, especially as you continue to add more books to your catalog.

Community

The Community tab on your KDP account page is a valuable resource for both new and experienced publishers. It includes Amazon announcements, user forums, and a comprehensive Help section.

While the forums can be a bit overwhelming for newcomers, they're a great place to learn from more experienced authors and pick up tips on everything from marketing strategies to troubleshooting account issues. Spending some time reading through these discussions can be surprisingly educational.

The Help section is also worth exploring, as it offers detailed tutorials and guides covering every aspect of the KDP platform, from formatting your manuscript to optimizing your book's sales page.

If you ever need direct support, you can find the Contact Us link within the Help tab in the Community section. This will guide you through a series of options to find the most relevant information before providing a way to reach out to Amazon's support team directly.

Marketing

The marketing tab on your KDP account page provides various tools to help you promote your books and reach a wider audience. Here's a quick overview of the options available:

• KDP Select – If you enroll your eBook in the KDP Select program, it becomes eligible for various promotional opportunities, including Kindle Unlimited and free or discounted pricing campaigns.

• Amazon Ads – This option allows you to run targeted ads on Amazon's platform, putting your book in front of potential readers who are already browsing for similar titles.

- Author Central – Use this tool to manage your author profile, track sales ranks, and view customer reviews, all from one convenient dashboard. It's also where you can add author bios, photos, and links to your other books.

- A+ Content – This feature lets you add enhanced content to your product detail pages, including images, text, and comparison tables, providing a more engaging experience for potential buyers.

- Run a Price Promotion – If your book is enrolled in KDP Select, you can create Kindle Countdown Deals or Free Book promotions directly from the Bookshelf page or within your book's listing.

- Nominate Your eBooks – You can also submit your books for special promotions, like Kindle Deals, which offer limited-time discounts, or Prime Reading, where select eBooks are available for free to Prime members.

Together, these tools provide a powerful set of options for boosting your book's visibility, building your author brand, and increasing your sales over time.

13

FORMATTING YOUR BOOK FILES FOR UPLOAD

Before you can upload your book to Amazon, you'll need to format the manuscript into a file type that the platform can read. There are a few different ways to do this, each with its own advantages depending on your needs and resources. The main options include formatting in Word, using Kindle Create, working with Vellum or Atticus, or hiring a professional formatter.

Formatting in Word

If you're looking for a straightforward, low-cost approach, you can format your book in Word and save it as a .DOCX file. This method gives you full control over the editing process and makes it easy to update your content as needed. To save your document in the correct format, simply choose the Save As option and select the location on your computer where you want to store the file. However, this approach has more limited formatting capabilities and may not produce the same polished, professional look as some of the dedicated formatting tools available.

Formatting in Kindle Create

Kindle Create is a free formatting tool provided by Amazon. It supports both Kindle eBooks and paperbacks, making it a convenient option if you're publishing through KDP. After downloading Kindle Create, open the program and select your .DOCX file to upload. The software offers features like clickable tables of contents, custom chapter headings, and built-in templates, allowing you to add a bit more polish to your manuscript without needing advanced design skills.

Formatting in Vellum or Atticus

For a more professional finish, Vellum and Atticus are excellent choices. Vellum is a highly regarded formatting tool for Mac users, known for its clean design and powerful features like custom drop caps, ornamental flourishes, box sets, and multi-platform exports. However, it comes with a one-time payment of around $199. For PC users, Atticus ($147) offers similar functionality with a user-friendly interface, making it a great alternative. Both programs simplify the formatting process, giving your book a polished, industry-standard appearance.

Hiring a Professional Formatter

If you find formatting too time-consuming or technically challenging, you can always hire a professional formatter through platforms like Fiverr or Upwork. These services vary widely in price and quality, so be sure to read reviews, check past work samples, and consider the number of revisions included before making a choice.

Getting your book files properly formatted is a critical part of the self-publishing process, but it doesn't have to be a daunting task. Whether you decide to handle the formatting yourself or hire a professional, the key is to make sure your book looks clean and professional on both Kindle and print devices.

Personally, I've found that investing in a dedicated formatting tool like Vellum has been a game-changer. It significantly speeds up the process, eliminating the need for constant back-and-forth with freelancers and reducing the chance of formatting errors. If you plan to publish multiple books, the one-time cost can quickly pay for itself.

14

DESIGNING YOUR BOOK COVER

Creating an eye-catching cover is one of the most important steps in the self-publishing process. A book's cover is often the first thing potential readers notice, and it plays a critical role in their decision to click on your book over the countless others available. Since readers can't physically pick up a digital book and flip through its pages, the cover becomes the primary way they assess the quality and appeal of your work.

There are a few different approaches to creating a professional-looking cover for your eBook or paperback book: designing it yourself using graphic design software, hiring a professional designer, or working with a dedicated design company. Each option has pros and cons, depending on your budget, design skills, and long-term publishing goals.

Before diving into these options, it's important to understand Amazon's specific cover requirements. For Kindle eBooks, Amazon recommends a height-to-width ratio of 1.6:1, with a minimum image height of 2,500 pixels to ensure your cover looks sharp on high-definition devices. The ideal dimensions are 2,560 x 1,600 pixels, and the file size must not exceed 50 MB. It's also important to avoid including any copyright-protected images, pricing information, or temporary promotions on your cover, as these can lead to your book being rejected or removed from the platform.

Designing Your Own Book Cover

Designing your own book cover can be a smart option—especially if you're just getting started, working with a tight budget, or enjoy the creative side of publishing. While hiring a professional designer is ideal for long-term branding and higher-stakes launches, many first-time authors find that creating their own covers helps them better understand what sells and how to communicate visually with readers.

If you're thinking of giving it a shot, start with user-friendly tools like Canva. Canva is free to use (with optional Pro features) and includes hundreds of customizable templates tailored specifically for Kindle and print books. You can drag and drop images, fonts, and backgrounds with ease, making it a perfect tool for beginners. Simply search "book cover" in the template library, and you'll find formats already sized for KDP specs.

If you want more creative control or plan to get more serious about design later, Adobe Photoshop is the industry standard. However, it comes with a learning curve and a monthly subscription, so it's best suited for those with existing experience or a strong desire to master the tool over time.

If you're designing your own cover, there are a few important things to keep in mind to make sure it looks professional and market-ready. Start by studying the top 20 books in your chosen category. Take note of common elements like font styles, color palettes, and image layouts. Your goal isn't to copy but to make your book look like it naturally belongs on the same shelf. Next, always use high-quality images—never blurry or pixelated ones. Canva offers a solid free photo library, or you can explore stock photo sites like Pexels, Unsplash, or Shutterstock if you're after more specific visuals.

Keep your design simple and clean. Avoid stuffing the cover with too much text or using overly decorative fonts that are hard to read. Clear and legible design is key—especially since most people will first see your cover as a tiny thumbnail on their phone.

It's also essential to match the overall style to your audience. For example, a children's book should look bright and playful, while a thriller might have a darker, more intense feel. The look should reflect the tone and emotion of the content inside.

If you want some creative control but aren't confident in your design skills, consider a hybrid approach—start with a Canva template, then hire someone on Fiverr or Upwork to fine-tune the final product for $20–$50. It's an affordable way to get a polished, professional-looking cover while still having a hand in the creative process.

Working with a Professional Designer

If you're serious about building a successful book business, investing in professional cover design is a smart move. Well-designed covers can dramatically increase your book's click-through rate and overall sales, making the initial investment well worth it.

To get started, platforms like Fiverr and Upwork are excellent places to find freelance designers. These sites let you browse portfolios, view past work, and read client reviews, making it easier to find a designer who understands your genre and can create covers that attract potential readers.

For beginners, Fiverr is a great starting point. You can quickly find designers offering affordable cover designs, sometimes as low as $5 per project. While the quality at this price point can vary, it's a good way to test different styles and get a feel for what you like. I recommend starting by ordering covers from three or four different designers, then combining the elements you like from each into a final design. With an investment of around $20, you can often come away with a polished, professional-looking cover.

As your business grows, you'll want to build a more long-term relationship with a dedicated designer. Upwork is a better platform for this, as it allows for more direct communication and ongoing collaboration. Over time, you can establish a working relationship with a designer who truly understands your brand, making the design process faster and more efficient.

For example, I now have a dedicated designer whom I can message at any time. They usually get back to me within a day or two with high-quality, unique cover designs. Currently, I pay them around $50 per cover, which I consider a worthwhile investment given the professional results and the time it saves me.

Working with a Professional Design Company

If you prefer a more polished, hands-off approach to cover design, working with a professional design company can be a great option. These companies often have teams of experienced designers who specialize in creating high-quality book covers that stand out in the crowded Amazon marketplace.

One service I've had good results with is 100 Covers. They offer professionally designed covers for around $100, but if you do a quick Google search for "100 Covers discount code," you can often find deals that bring the price down to $50. They typically have a turnaround time of about one to two weeks and offer unlimited revisions, which is a huge plus if you want to fine-tune the final design.

This approach can be particularly effective if you order your cover early in the writing process. By the time you finish your manuscript, your cover will likely be ready as well, allowing you to hit the publish button as soon as you're done writing. It's a cost-effective solution if you're not ready to invest in design skills or hire a dedicated designer just yet.

Creating Paperback Covers

For paperback books, the cover file must include the front cover, spine, and back cover, all combined into a single PDF file. The exact dimensions depend on your book's page count and trim size, as the spine width will vary based on the number of pages. To simplify this process, Amazon offers a free Paperback File Setup Calculator and cover templates, which you can access here: https://kdp.amazon.com/en_US/cover-calculator.

If you've already created an eBook cover, converting it into a full paperback cover is a relatively straightforward and cost-effective process. One option is to hire a freelancer on platforms like Fiverr.com, where you can often find someone to handle the conversion for as little as $5.

Alternatively, you can take a DIY approach using Canva.com. Simply download the template from Amazon, then add your spine and back cover text directly in Canva. This approach can save you money and give you more creative control over the final design.

Before I found a dedicated designer, I took a hybrid approach—I would use 100 Covers for the front cover, which typically cost around $100 (or less with a discount code), and then create the spine and back cover myself. This method saved both time and money, reducing the need for constant back-and-forth communication on Fiverr and speeding up the overall design process.

What Makes a Great Book Cover?

Creating a successful book cover is a blend of art and strategy. It's about capturing the essence of your book while also grabbing the attention of potential readers as they scroll through a crowded marketplace. While there's no single formula for a perfect cover, a few key principles tend to hold true:

1. Theme Alignment – Your cover should visually capture the tone and subject of your book. It's essentially a one-image summary, giving readers an instant sense of what to expect.

2. Clear and Readable Title – Choose a bold, legible font that stands out against the background. The title should be easy to read, even at thumbnail size, with strong color contrast to ensure it pops off the page.

3. Professional Appearance – A polished, high-quality cover signals to potential buyers that your book is worth their time. It sets the tone for the reading experience and builds trust before a single word is read.

4. Scroll-Stopping Power – This is the ultimate test. Your cover needs to be visually striking enough to make someone stop, take a closer look, and click to learn more. It's a tough balance to strike, but when done right, it can significantly boost your book's chances of success.

Let's try a little creative exercise. Without peeking at the titles, take a closer look at the three covers in front of you:

For the one on the far left, what kind of story or theme do you think it's hinting at based on the imagery and design elements?

Next, check out the middle cover. Can you identify the types of food featured? What kind of mood or tone do you think the designer was aiming for?

Finally, consider the cover on the far right. What vibe does it give off? Does it hint at a particular genre or topic?

Once you've made your guesses, flip to the next page to see how close you were.

Without even glancing at the titles, you can probably make some solid guesses about the themes of the first two covers. The leftmost one, with its honeycomb pattern and bee imagery, clearly points to something related to beekeeping or honey production. The middle cover, with its close-up of cookies and brownies, practically shouts baking or desserts. These covers do a great job of visually representing their content, making it easy for potential readers to immediately understand what the book is about.

The last cover, however, is a different story. Without any clear visual cues, it's harder to guess that the book is actually about finance and retirement planning. The lack of relevant imagery makes it less effective, as it doesn't provide an instant visual connection to the topic, which can be a missed opportunity when trying to capture a reader's attention.

Here are the full titles:

• Beekeeping for Beginners: The New Complete Guide to Raise a Healthy and Thriving Beehive

- 100 Cookies: The Baking Book for Every Kitchen, with Classic Cookies, Novel Treats, Brownies, Bars, and More

- Looking Ahead: Life, Family, Wealth and Business After 55

Up for another quick challenge? Take a look at the two covers side by side. Without overthinking it, which one catches your eye first – the cover on the left or the one on the right?

 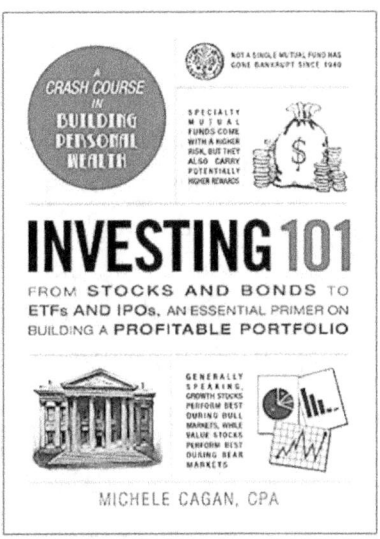

If you picked the right one, you've got an eye for effective design. Both books are about investing, but the cover on the right clearly stands out with its use of financial symbols and visually appealing design elements. It's a great example of how the right imagery and layout can instantly communicate the topic, making it more likely to grab a potential reader's attention.

Of course, not all covers are created equal. Let's look at an example of what to avoid—a once-popular template design that now screams "amateur." If you want your book to stand out, it's best to avoid these cookie-cutter designs that can make your work look generic.

Take a look at the collection of covers below, all using a similar template under the keyword "Puppy Training for Beginners." While many of them blend together, a few stand out from the pack. Can you spot the ones that break the mold and avoid the typical, overused design elements? Consider factors like color choice, image quality, and font style as you try to pick out the more distinctive covers.

Flip to the next page to see if you spotted the standouts.

Did you choose numbers three and six? Well done! These covers stand out from the rest with their distinctive designs and clear messaging. Not only do they break away from the overused template, but their strong visual appeal is also backed up by impressive Best Seller Ranks (BSR) on Amazon, confirming that they're connecting well with readers.

Best-Selling Book Covers

Take a moment to check out these best-selling covers.

They serve as great examples of how the right design can perfectly capture the essence of a book's topic. Notice how the images, fonts, and color schemes work together to create a cohesive, eye-catching final product. This kind of visual harmony can make a book feel polished and professional, elevating it above the competition.

Final Thoughts

Despite the old saying, readers absolutely judge a book by its cover. After pouring your time and effort into writing your manuscript, the last thing you want is for it to be overlooked because of a poorly designed cover. To stand out in the crowded Amazon marketplace, your book needs a polished, attention-grabbing cover that instantly communicates its value.

As you gain more experience in publishing, you'll start to develop an eye for what makes a cover truly effective. You'll learn to recognize the design elements that work for your niche and build a strong collaborative relationship with a designer who understands your brand. This kind of experience will pay off in the long run, helping you create covers that perfectly capture the spirit of your books and attract the right readers.

15

UPLOADING YOUR EBOOK

Uploading your book to Amazon is one of the simplest steps in the self-publishing process. Compared to the effort it takes to write, edit, and format your manuscript, this part is quick and straightforward. Once you have your KDP account set up, the entire upload process can be completed in just a few minutes.

To get started, log into your KDP account. You'll land on your personal dashboard, which defaults to the Bookshelf tab. This is where you'll manage all of your published books, track sales, and add new titles.

At the top of the page, you'll see the heading "Create. Manage. Publish." Directly beneath it, you'll find a section titled "Create a new title or series." Here, Amazon lets you know that you can publish your work in various formats, including eBooks, paperbacks, hardcovers, and Kindle Vella stories (Kindle Vella is Amazon's platform for serialized stories, released in short episodes that readers unlock with tokens). If you plan to publish a series, you can also create an Amazon series page to keep all of your books grouped together.

To start the upload process, click the large "+ Create" button. This will open a page titled "What would you like to create?" Inside the Kindle eBook section, click the "Create eBook" button. This will take you to a new screen with three separate pages, starting with the "Kindle eBook Details" page, where you'll enter the essential information about your book.

Language

The first field you'll encounter when uploading your book is the language selection. By default, this is usually set to the primary language of the Amazon marketplace you're publishing in. For example, if you're using Amazon's U.S. site, the language will default to English. However, Amazon supports many languages, including Afrikaans, Arabic, Danish, Dutch, Finnish, French, German, Italian, Japanese, Portuguese, Spanish, Swedish, and more.

Expanding into other languages can be a smart long-term strategy, allowing you to reach a much wider audience. Translating your books can significantly boost your sales, especially in large markets like Spanish, German, and French. For example, I decided to translate one of my best-selling books into these three languages. The Spanish and German versions sell steadily each month, but the French version has been a standout success, becoming my fourth best-selling book this year.

That said, translations can be expensive, so I recommend considering this step only after you've built a solid foundation with at least ten books and a consistent monthly income of around $1,000. This approach reduces your risk and ensures you have the financial stability to experiment with new markets.

Book Title

The next step is to enter your book's title. This is where you'll add the main title and, if you have one, a subtitle. Keep in mind that while you can change your Kindle book title at any time after publication, you cannot change the title of a paperback once it's been published. This is because Amazon requires the title and subtitle on your paperback's cover to exactly match the title you enter here.

To avoid any issues, it's a good idea to come up with a single title that works for both your Kindle and paperback versions. This keeps your branding consistent and reduces the chances of your book being rejected during the approval process.

When entering your title, it's best to separate the main title and subtitle with a hyphen, like this: The Ketogenic Cook Book - A Beginner's Guide to Learning the Keto Diet. I prefer to include the subtitle directly in the main title box rather than using the separate subtitle field. This is because the subtitle field is marked as optional, and it's unclear whether Amazon factors those words into its search algorithm. By keeping everything in the main title, you can be more confident that the keywords you've included will be taken into account, potentially improving your book's visibility.

Book Title	Enter your title as it appears on the book cover. This field cannot be changed after your book is published. Learn more about book titles.
	Book Title
	The Ketogenic Cook Book - A Beginner' Guide To Learning The Keto Diet
	Subtitle (Optional)

Series

If your book is part of a series, you can include it in a series listing to make it easier for readers to find your other titles. This feature allows you to create a dedicated series page on Amazon, where all related books are grouped together, making it simpler for readers to discover and purchase multiple titles within the same series. Once the setup is complete, any linked formats for the title will automatically be added to the series, allowing readers to view all available formats on a single page and choose the one that suits them best.

Creating a series also lets you establish a reading order, which can be helpful if your books follow a chronological storyline or share common characters and settings. However, you can also leave the titles unordered if the books can be read in any order. It's important to keep your series consistent, with related themes, characters, or settings, as this helps readers understand what to expect from each title and builds a sense of continuity.

If you plan to offer your series in multiple languages, it's a good idea to create separate series pages for each language version. This ensures that readers can easily find all the titles in their preferred language without confusion. Also, avoid adding duplicate content to the same series, as readers purchasing all the titles expect each book to be unique. If they encounter repeated material, it can lead to negative reviews, which can hurt your long-term sales.

At the beginning of your self-publishing journey, you probably won't have a series yet, so there's no need to worry about this step right away. However, it's a good feature to keep in mind as you expand your catalog over time.

Edition Number

The edition number field is where you can indicate which version of your book you're publishing. This is typically used if you're releasing a second or updated edition of an existing title. For example, if you originally published a book and then made significant revisions or added new content, you could label the updated version as the second edition.

However, this field is optional, and you can leave it blank if you're publishing the first version of your book.

From my experience, it's often better to publish a brand new book rather than simply updating an old one. This approach gives you two separate listings on Amazon, effectively doubling your earning potential. This can be particularly useful for books that are designed to be updated annually, like "The 2023 Fitness Guide" and "The 2024 Fitness Guide."

By releasing a fresh edition as a standalone title, you not only capture the attention of new readers but also give past buyers a reason to purchase the latest version, potentially boosting your overall sales.

Author

The author field is where you enter the primary author's name, which can be either your real name, a pen name, or a brand name. This name will be displayed on your book's product page and cannot be changed once the book is published, so choose carefully. If you plan to build a brand around a specific pen name, make sure it fits the tone and style of the books you intend to publish.

Contributors

The contributors section is where you can add the names of any additional people involved in creating the book, such as co-authors, editors, illustrators, or translators. Just keep in mind that if you're the primary author, your name should only appear in the author field, not in the contributors section as well. This helps keep your listings clean and avoids any confusion for potential buyers.

Description

The description section is one of the most important parts of your book's product page, as it's your main chance to convince potential readers to make a purchase. This section allows you to provide a summary of your book, highlight its main themes, and set the tone for what readers can expect.

You can enhance your description using basic HTML or Amazon's built-in formatting tools, which allow you to add elements like italics, underlines, bullet points, and numbered lists. This helps break up the text, making it more visually appealing and easier to read. However, be careful not to overuse these features, as a cluttered description can be off-putting to potential buyers.

When writing your description, aim to keep it clear, compelling, and concise. Focus on capturing the main idea or plot without overwhelming readers with unnecessary detail. A strong first sentence is crucial, as the first few lines are often all a potential buyer will see before they have to click "Read more."

Additionally, Amazon has specific guidelines for what you can and cannot include in your description. Avoid using personal contact information, time-sensitive promotions, or any content that could be considered offensive. Also, don't include reviews or testimonials, as these are not allowed and can lead to your book being rejected.

One lesser-known trick used by successful authors is to incorporate relevant keywords directly into the description. This not only helps with Amazon's internal search algorithms but also makes the text more engaging and informative. For example, if your book is about healthy eating and plant-based diets, you might write something like:

"Ready to transform your health and embrace a vibrant lifestyle? Discover the power of plant-based eating and learn how to nourish your body with delicious, nutrient-rich meals that boost energy and support long-term wellness."

This approach allows you to naturally include keywords without resorting to a simple list, which can feel spammy and unprofessional. Remember, your description is your first real opportunity to sell your book, so make every word count.

Publishing Rights

In the publishing rights section, you'll need to indicate whether you own the copyright for your book or if it's a public domain work. If you've written the book yourself or hired a writer to create original content, select the first option, which confirms that you hold the necessary rights to publish the work. Under U.S. copyright law, your work is automatically protected as soon as you create it, so you don't need to register it for copyright right away. This is something you might consider later if your book starts generating significant revenue, but it's not essential in the early stages.

The second option, "This is a public domain work," is for books that are freely available for anyone to reproduce, like classic literature that is no longer under copyright protection. However, this approach is generally not recommended if you're trying to build a long-term brand, as it can be challenging to stand out and earn a consistent income with public domain content.

Keywords

Choosing the right keywords for your book is a critical part of optimizing its visibility on Amazon. While the title and subtitle of your book offer some keyword opportunities, the backend keyword section is where you can really expand your reach. Amazon gives you seven keyword boxes, and there are two main approaches to filling them: using a single, targeted keyword in each box or cramming multiple keywords into a single box.

From my experience and based on tests from other publishers, it seems that using fewer, more focused keywords in each box is the better approach. When you stuff each box with multiple keywords, it can dilute the relevance and reduce the impact of each term. If you've already chosen a strong title and subtitle, you shouldn't need to overstuff these boxes. Instead, aim for precise, highly relevant keywords that clearly describe your book's topic. If you have leftover keywords that don't fit naturally in your title or description, this is the place to use them.

To find these keywords, start by paying attention to the suggestions that appear in Amazon's search field when you start typing. These suggestions are based on real customer searches, making them a valuable source of keyword ideas. You can also look at the keywords used in other successful books in your genre for inspiration.

However, it's important to avoid certain types of keywords that Amazon discourages. These include:

• Words that are already included in your book's title, subtitle, or author name

• Overly subjective claims like "best book ever" or "must-read"

• Time-sensitive phrases like "new," "on sale," or "available now"

• Generic terms like "book" or "novel" that don't add any real value

• References to Amazon programs like Kindle Unlimited or KDP Select

Categories

Selecting the right categories for your book is another critical part of the upload process. When setting up both your Kindle eBook and paperback versions, you'll have the opportunity to choose three categories for each. Interestingly, the available category options differ between Kindle eBooks and paperbacks, which actually works to your advantage. By selecting different categories for each version, you can increase your book's visibility across multiple sections on Amazon, giving it a better chance of being discovered by a wider audience.

Age & Grade Range

This is primarily for children's books, allowing parents and teachers to sort books by the appropriate age level. If you're publishing a book for adults, you can safely skip this section, as it won't have any impact on your book's visibility or sales.

Pre-Orders

Pre-orders are a popular strategy among fiction authors, especially those writing series, as they can build anticipation and encourage early sales from dedicated readers. This approach is particularly effective if you have a fan base that's eager to get their hands on the next installment of your series. Some authors even go as far as loading several books as pre-orders at once, especially if they plan to release a new title every month or two. When a reader pre-orders one book in your series, Amazon will automatically notify them when the next one becomes available, creating a steady stream of sales.

To set up a pre-order, you'll need to choose between "I am ready to release my book now" or "Make my Kindle eBook available for Pre-order." It's important to note that this option is only available for Kindle eBooks, not paperbacks. If you're releasing both a Kindle and paperback version, it's a good idea to upload the paperback a few days before the Kindle release, as the approval process for paperbacks can sometimes take longer.

That said, pre-orders are less common in nonfiction publishing. Personally, I've never used pre-orders for my nonfiction books, and a few of my publishing friends who have experimented with them didn't notice a significant boost in sales. So, if you're focused on nonfiction, this is one less thing to worry about.

Second Page

Once you've completed the first page of the KDP setup, you can either save as a draft or save and continue to move on to the second page, where you'll upload your manuscript. It's a good idea to double-check all the information you've entered, as some fields, like the book title and author name, cannot be changed once the book is published. This is a critical step, so take a moment to make sure everything is accurate before moving on.

Digital Rights Management

The next section you'll encounter is the Digital Rights Management (DRM) setting. According to Amazon, DRM is designed to prevent unauthorized sharing of your Kindle book file. It essentially locks the file, restricting how it can be copied or transferred.

However, some authors choose to leave the DRM box unchecked, opting to make their books more shareable. The idea is that if a reader enjoys your work and wants to share it with others, this can actually help spread the word about your book, potentially leading to more sales in the long run. It's worth noting that even with DRM enabled, readers can still lend your book to another user for a short period or gift it through the Kindle store.

One thing to keep in mind is that once your book is published, you can't change the DRM setting, so it's a decision you'll need to make upfront. Personally, I tend to leave the DRM box unchecked, as this is the default option and likely reflects Amazon's preference. At the end of the day, if someone is determined to find a way to share your book without paying for it, DRM won't necessarily stop them, so it might be better to focus on building a loyal reader base instead.

Upload Book Manuscript

Once you've made it to the second page of the KDP setup, it's time to upload your manuscript. This is a straightforward process. Simply click the yellow "Upload eBook manuscript" button and select your file from your computer. Depending on how you formatted your book, this file could be a .DOCX from Word, a .KPF from Kindle Create, or a .EPUB from Vellum or Atticus.

One advantage of the KDP platform is that you can upload a new version of your manuscript at any time. This flexibility allows you to make updates, fix errors, or add new content whenever needed. If Amazon detects potential spelling errors in your manuscript, it will display an alert. You can click on each highlighted word to decide whether it's a genuine mistake or simply an unrecognized term, like a piece of slang or a unique name. If it's a real error, you'll need to correct it in your original file, reformat if necessary, and then re-upload the updated version. If the word is correct, you can simply hit the "ignore" button and move on.

Kindle eBook Cover

The next step in the process is to upload your book cover. Amazon provides two options here: you can either use the Cover Creator tool or upload a pre-made cover file.

While the Cover Creator is a convenient option, I strongly recommend against using it, as the designs can come across as generic and unprofessional. Instead, it's better to upload a cover you've already created or had professionally designed. Make sure your file is in JPG or TIFF format, as these are the only formats Amazon accepts.

Once you've uploaded your cover, you'll need to click the "Launch Previewer" button to check how your manuscript and cover look together. This is a crucial step, as it's your final chance to catch formatting issues or design flaws before your book goes live. Keep in mind that Amazon's system may take a few minutes to process your files, sometimes up to ten or twenty minutes, so don't worry if it takes a little while.

Once the preview loads, take the time to carefully review each page to ensure everything looks the way you intended. If you spot any problems, you can go back, make the necessary changes, and re-upload your files.

ISBN

An ISBN (International Standard Book Number) is a unique identifier used to track and catalog books. While Kindle eBooks don't require an ISBN, paperbacks do, and Amazon conveniently provides a free ISBN for you to use. This is a great option if you plan to exclusively publish on Amazon, as it saves you the cost and hassle of purchasing your own.

While owning your own ISBNs gives you full control over your publication and allows you to sell your book on other platforms, it can be expensive and isn't always necessary, especially when you're just starting out. Most of your sales will likely come from Amazon anyway, so it's better to focus your time and resources on creating and promoting new books rather than worrying about ISBN ownership.

If I were starting again, I wouldn't bother purchasing ISBNs or trying to publish my books widely. Instead, I'd stick to Amazon's free ISBNs, get my books published quickly, and then move on to the next project. This approach aligns perfectly with the 80/20 rule—focusing your efforts where they'll have the most impact.

Third Page

Once you've reviewed and approved your manuscript and cover files, you can move on to the third and final page of the KDP setup process. It's worth noting that the information on this page, including your book files, can be updated at any time, giving you flexibility if you need to make changes down the road.

KDP Select Enrollment

At the top of this final page, you'll find the KDP Select enrollment section. We covered this earlier, but here's a quick refresher. KDP Select is Amazon's program that makes your book eligible for Kindle Unlimited (KU), a subscription service where readers pay a monthly fee for unlimited access to eligible eBooks. To participate, you need to enroll your book in KDP Select, which locks you into a ninety-day exclusivity period for the Kindle version of your book. During this time, you can't publish the eBook on any other platform, though you're free to distribute the paperback version wherever you like.

While the payout for Kindle Unlimited reads is typically around half a cent per page (or about one penny for every two pages), this isn't the primary reason most authors choose to enroll in KDP Select. The real advantage comes from the promotional tools Amazon offers as part of the program:

• Free Book Promotions – You can make your book available for free for up to five days per ninety-day enrollment period. This can be a great way to boost visibility, gather reviews, and drive more paperback sales.

- Kindle Countdown Deals – If your book is priced between $2.99 and $24.99, you can run Kindle Countdown Deals that temporarily reduce the price of your book, creating a sense of urgency and encouraging readers to buy now.

While the exclusivity requirement might seem limiting, it often makes sense for new authors to enroll in KDP Select, at least for the first ninety days. Amazon is more likely to promote books that are part of its own program, potentially giving you a much-needed visibility boost as you launch your first titles.

Territories

In the Territories section, you'll need to decide where your book will be available for purchase. The simplest and most common choice is to select "All territories (worldwide rights)," which ensures your book is available on all of Amazon's regional sites. This includes major markets like the U.S., U.K., Germany, France, Spain, Italy, Japan, Netherlands, Brazil, Mexico, Canada, India, and Australia, among others. This is the default setting for a reason, as it gives your book the widest possible reach without any additional effort.

Primary Marketplace

Next, you'll choose your Primary Marketplace. This is the Amazon site where you expect to make the majority of your sales. By default, this is usually set to Amazon.com (the U.S. site), and I recommend leaving it that way unless you have a specific reason to focus on a different market. In my experience, around 95% of sales come from the U.S. marketplace, making it the most profitable choice for most authors.

Pricing, Royalty & Distribution

One of the advantages of self-publishing on Amazon is the flexibility you have in setting your book's price. Amazon offers two main royalty options for Kindle eBooks, each with its own pros and cons depending on your pricing strategy and the file size of your book.

If you price your book between 99 cents and $2.98, or $10 and above, you'll earn a 35% royalty. This lower royalty tier has the benefit of no delivery fees, making it a good choice for shorter, lower-priced books or those with large file sizes, like image-heavy guides or picture books. For your first book, I recommend launching at 99 cents for the first month to encourage more downloads and reviews.

The 70% royalty option is available for books priced between $2.99 and $9.99, which is the sweet spot for most Kindle eBooks. However, this tier comes with a delivery fee of 15 cents per megabyte, which is deducted from your royalties. After your initial launch period, it's a good idea to raise your price to $2.99 or higher to take advantage of this better payout rate.

Amazon automatically converts your book's price to local currencies for international markets, which can simplify the pricing process. However, you still have the option to set specific prices for different regions if you want to adjust for local purchasing power or market conditions. Remember, you can adjust your book's pricing at any time.

For your first book, it's smart to start with a 99-cent price under the 35% royalty option. This lower price encourages early sales, improves your book's rank, and helps you collect those crucial first reviews. After about a month, once your book has gained some traction and gathered positive feedback, you can raise the price to $2.99 to take advantage of the 70% royalty tier.

If you don't have a large social media following, enrolling your first book in **KDP Select** can be a smart move. This allows Kindle Unlimited members to borrow your book, potentially generating more reviews and improving your book's visibility over time. While the per-page payout is modest, these borrows can help your book gain traction, which is crucial in the early stages.

It's natural for new authors to feel hesitant about pricing their work too low, especially after putting in so much effort. However, it's important to remember that the Kindle market is extremely competitive, with thousands of self-published authors vying for the same audience. Many of these authors have been building their reader bases for years, so starting at a lower price can help you stand out and attract those crucial early readers.

As your audience grows and you establish a track record, you can gradually increase your prices, but in the beginning, it's all about gaining momentum and building a base of loyal readers.

Book Lending

Book lending is a feature that allows Kindle users to share their purchased eBooks with friends or family for a period of fourteen days. During this time, the lender temporarily loses access to the book until the loan period ends. This option is only available for Kindle books purchased through Amazon and can be a way for your work to reach a wider audience.

If you've purchased a copy of your own book, you also have the option to lend it, but keep in mind that each title can only be loaned once, and these loans do not generate royalty payments. By default, all books published through KDP are enrolled in the lending program, but if you choose the 35% royalty option, you have the flexibility to opt out by unchecking the box in the "Book Lending" section during the setup process. However, this option is not available for books enrolled in the 70% royalty tier or those included in another distribution program.

Personally, I've chosen to disable book lending for my titles. While I enabled it in the past, I found that the feature isn't as widely used as it once was, and it doesn't provide the same income potential as a straightforward sale or KDP Select borrow. My preference is to either have readers borrow my books through Kindle Unlimited or purchase them outright, as both options provide a direct financial benefit.

Publishing Your eBook

Once you've filled out all the necessary sections for your Kindle eBook, the final step is to hit the "Publish Your Kindle eBook" button at the bottom of the page. After clicking this, your book will enter Amazon's review process, which can take up to seventy-two hours before it goes live on the site.

16

UPLOADING YOUR PAPERBACK

Once your Kindle eBook is live, you can create a paperback version to expand your book's reach and cater to readers who prefer physical copies. To get started, log into your KDP account, find your published Kindle book on your Bookshelf, and click the "+ Create Paperback" link next to the title.

Many of the fields from your Kindle eBook setup will be automatically pre-filled for your convenience, but you'll still have the option to edit most of them. One section unique to the paperback setup is the Adult Content field. Here, you'll need to indicate whether your book contains language, situations, or images that might not be appropriate for readers under eighteen. Unless your book is explicitly intended for mature audiences, it's generally best to select "NO" in this section, as this will prevent Amazon from restricting your book's visibility.

Second Page

After completing the first page, click "Save & Continue" to move on to the second page. Unlike eBooks, paperbacks require an ISBN. You can either purchase your own ISBNs from Bowker.com or opt for Amazon's free KDP ISBN. For now, I recommend sticking with the free option, as it keeps things simple and reduces upfront costs.

You'll also see a Publication Date field, which is only relevant if your book has been previously published on another platform. If this is your book's first publication, you can skip this field, as Amazon will automatically assign the publication date once your book goes live.

Keep in mind that, unlike Kindle eBooks, paperbacks cannot be submitted for pre-order, so you'll need to have everything ready before you hit the publish button.

Paperback Options

When setting up your paperback book, you'll have a few important choices to make regarding the interior, trim size, bleed settings, cover finish, and file formats. Here's a quick overview of what to expect:

Ink and Paper Types:

• Black and white interior with cream paper: Typically used for fiction and memoirs. It has a paper weight of 55 pounds and offers a slightly more traditional, premium feel.

• Black and white interior with white paper: Amazon's default option, often used for nonfiction and reference books. It also has a 55-pound paper weight and provides a clean, bright background for text.

• Standard color interior with white paper: A more affordable option for books with color elements, but not ideal for full-color images. It also uses 55-pound paper.

• Premium color interior with white paper: Best for books with full-color elements, like children's picture books, photography collections, or cookbooks. It uses heavier 60-pound paper for a more professional look.

Trim Size: This refers to the physical dimensions of your book. The most common sizes for self-published nonfiction are 5x8 inches and 6x9 inches. Choosing the right trim size can impact your book's printing costs and overall feel, so consider your genre and target audience when making this decision.

Bleed Settings: Bleed refers to the practice of printing your book's pages right up to the edge, without any white margins. This is typically only necessary if your book contains full-page images or graphics that extend to the edge of the page. Most text-based books will use the "no bleed" setting.

Paperback Cover Finish: Amazon offers two cover finish options: glossy and matte. Glossy covers have a shiny, reflective finish that can make colors pop, while matte covers have a softer, more muted look that many authors prefer for a premium feel. Personally, I use matte for all my books, as it gives them a more professional, polished appearance.

Manuscript File: In this section, you'll upload the file for your paperback book. Amazon supports various file formats, including PDF, DOC, DOCX, HTML, and RTF. I recommend using PDF for the cleanest and most consistent formatting.

Book Cover File: Unlike your Kindle eBook cover, the paperback version includes a front cover, spine, and back cover in a single print-ready PDF file. Make sure your cover file matches your chosen trim size and includes the correct spine width based on your page count.

Launch Preview: Once you've uploaded your manuscript and cover, you'll have the opportunity to "Launch Previewer" and review how your book will look in print. Amazon's preview tool lets you check for formatting errors, image quality, and overall layout, so take your time with this step. It may take a few minutes for Amazon to process the files, but this step is crucial for ensuring your final product meets your quality standards.

Summary: Before moving on to the final page, you'll see a Summary section that provides a final look at your interior and cover files, along with the estimated printing costs. This cost will be deducted automatically from the sale price of your book, so it's a good idea to make sure everything looks perfect before moving forward.

Third Page

As you move to the third page of the paperback setup, you'll come across the Territories section, which is similar to what you encountered when uploading your Kindle version. Here, you have the option to make your book available worldwide or restrict it to specific regions. It's always a good idea to select "All Territories (Worldwide Rights)" to maximize your book's reach, allowing readers from around the globe to purchase your paperback.

Next, you'll see the Primary Marketplace field. This determines the main Amazon store where your book will be listed and promoted. By default, it will be set to the marketplace based on your location, but I recommend switching this to Amazon.com if it's not already selected. This is because the vast majority of book sales come from the U.S., regardless of where you live, making it the most profitable choice for most authors.

Pricing, Royalty, & Distribution

Paperback books on Amazon earn a 60% royalty, calculated after subtracting Amazon's share and the printing costs. These printing costs vary based on factors like page count, trim size, and color options (black and white vs. color). Unlike Kindle eBooks, paperbacks have higher production expenses, so it's important to set your price accordingly to ensure you're earning a reasonable profit per sale.

It's also worth noting that while your paperback will be available to international buyers, it won't have the same global reach as a Kindle eBook. Amazon only prints and ships paperbacks from certain regions, which can limit availability in some markets.

Publish Your Paperback Book

Once you've set the price for your paperback, the final step is to click the "Publish Your Paperback Book" button. Keep in mind that, unlike Kindle eBooks, which are usually approved within a few hours, paperback books can take several days to pass Amazon's review process. This is because Amazon needs to verify that the file you've uploaded will print correctly and meet their quality standards. Once approved, your paperback will go live on Amazon's website, ready to be discovered by readers around the world.

Request Proof Copies

Once your paperback is published, you have the option to order proof copies directly from your KDP dashboard. These copies are sold at a discounted rate, allowing you to physically review the book before it's widely available to customers. Proof copies are a great way to check for formatting issues, paper quality, and overall presentation, ensuring your book meets your standards before it reaches readers.

17

GETTING REVIEWS FOR YOUR BOOK

Reviews are a critical part of your book's success on Amazon, serving multiple important functions. First, they build credibility and trust. When potential buyers see that others have enjoyed your book, it reassures them that their purchase will be worthwhile. Think about your own shopping habits—when was the last time you bought something on Amazon with zero or just a handful of reviews? Probably not often. That social proof can be the deciding factor in converting a casual browser into a paying customer.

Reviews also play a significant role in Amazon's algorithm, directly impacting your book's visibility and ranking. Books with more positive reviews are more likely to appear in search results, recommendation lists, and "Customers also bought" sections. This increased visibility can drive organic sales without the need for heavy advertising, making reviews one of the most cost-effective marketing tools at your disposal.

They directly influence the conversion rate of a book as well. Even if your book has a great cover and compelling description, readers are more likely to hit the "Buy" button if they see a solid number of positive reviews. In short, reviews aren't just a nice bonus—they're a crucial part of your book's long-term success.

Types of Reviews

Not all book reviews on Amazon carry the same weight, both in the eyes of potential buyers and Amazon's algorithm. Understanding the different types of reviews can help you encourage the ones that have the most impact on your book's success.

First, there are **unverified reviews**. These come from readers who haven't purchased the book through Amazon, so their reviews lack the "Verified Purchase" badge. While these still contribute to your overall star rating, they tend to carry less influence. Potential buyers often perceive them as less trustworthy, and Amazon's algorithm may give them less weight when determining your book's ranking and visibility in search results.

Next, you have **verified reviews**, which are far more valuable. These are left by readers who have actually bought your book through Amazon, and their reviews include the "Verified Purchase" tag. This badge signals to potential buyers that the feedback is based on a genuine purchase, making it more credible and impactful. Amazon's algorithm also likely weighs these reviews more heavily, potentially improving your book's discoverability.

Then there's the matter of **review length and detail**. While a short, generic comment like "I liked the book" is better than no review at all, it lacks the depth to influence buying decisions significantly. In contrast, a more thoughtful, in-depth review where the reader shares specific insights, like how the book helped them or what they found particularly valuable, can be a game-changer. These detailed reviews not only provide potential buyers with a clearer sense of the book's quality but also offer valuable SEO benefits. For instance, if a reader mentions terms like "ideal for container gardening," "perfect for balcony gardens," or "small space vegetable guide" in their review of a gardening book, these keywords can help boost your book's visibility in Amazon's search results, as they closely match what potential buyers are likely searching for.

Moving up the ladder, **image reviews** add another layer of credibility. When readers upload pictures of your physical book, it provides social proof that the book is real, professionally produced, and worth the purchase. This can significantly increase your book's perceived value and conversion rates, as potential buyers get a more tangible sense of what they're getting.

Finally, there are **video reviews**, which are the gold standard. These reviews offer the most credibility, as they allow potential buyers to see the book in someone's hands, hear genuine feedback, and get a firsthand sense of the book's quality. This type of review can dramatically boost your conversion rates, as it builds the strongest possible trust between the reviewer and prospective buyers.

The Perfect Review

The perfect review on Amazon combines multiple powerful elements to maximize its impact:

It starts with a verified purchase tag, confirming the reviewer genuinely bought the book, which immediately boosts credibility. The review itself is detailed and personal, offering specific insights into how the book helped or inspired the reader. Instead of just saying, "I liked this book," it might include specifics like, "This guide on container gardening completely transformed my small balcony into a thriving green space. The step-by-step planting tips and easy-to-follow illustrations made the process straightforward, even for a beginner like me. Within weeks, I was growing my first cherry tomatoes and fresh herbs. It's become my go-to reference for small space gardening."

To take it a step further, the reviewer includes photos of their balcony garden, showcasing the real-world results they achieved using the book's advice. This visual proof reinforces the book's value and gives potential buyers a tangible sense of the book's effectiveness.

Finally, the perfect review might also include a video, where the reviewer talks through their experience, flips through the pages of the book, and shows the plants they've grown as a result. This combination of text, images, and video offers the highest level of social proof, building maximum trust and significantly increasing the likelihood of converting a potential buyer into a paying customer.

Together, these elements create a highly persuasive review that not only boosts the book's credibility but also positively impacts its ranking in Amazon's search results, thanks to the rich, keyword-filled text.

Getting Reviews Without Getting Banned

While it might be tempting to ask friends and family for reviews, it's important to tread carefully. Amazon's guidelines explicitly discourage this, as they consider reviews from people with a personal connection to the author as potentially biased. To avoid running afoul of these rules, focus on building a broader, unbiased reader base.

Instead of directly asking friends or family for reviews, you can encourage them to support your book in other ways, like sharing it on social media, recommending it to their networks, or even purchasing a copy for themselves. These actions can still boost your book's visibility and sales without violating Amazon's policies.

Ethical Ways to Get More Reviews

Using Booksprout for Reviews

Booksprout is a popular platform for gathering early reviews, even though they will typically be unverified on Amazon. While this means the reviews won't have the "Verified Purchase" badge, which carries more weight, they still count toward your overall star rating and can improve your book's visibility. This is a solid starting point, especially if you're launching your first book and want to build some initial credibility.

Here's how it works. You start by uploading the PDF of your book to Booksprout. Readers then have the opportunity to claim a free copy in exchange for an honest review, which they typically post within a few weeks of downloading the book. Once your book is live on Amazon, you can send a follow-up message through Booksprout, gently reminding these readers to leave their reviews. The platform provides a convenient dashboard to track who has downloaded your book and whether they've left a review, making it easier to follow up if needed.

It's important to keep in mind that readers on Booksprout can be quite critical, so make sure your book is polished and ready for public scrutiny before sharing it. While this might seem daunting, it's actually a positive thing in the long run. A mix of glowing and more reserved reviews creates a more authentic overall rating, which potential buyers are likely to trust. It also shows that your reviews aren't just from overly generous friends and family, which can increase your book's credibility.

However, don't expect a flood of reviews. Booksprout is great for getting those first few, but most authors only receive a handful of reviews from each campaign. Still, these initial reviews can be valuable for building early momentum.

Timing your Booksprout campaign is also important. Ideally, you should launch it a few days before your book goes live on Amazon, so you can have a wave of reviews ready to post as soon as your listing is live. This early momentum can help boost your book's ranking and visibility, giving it a stronger start.

While Booksprout does offer a free tier, their paid plan (starting at $9/month) includes helpful extras like automated review reminders and access to a larger pool of potential reviewers. If you plan to publish multiple books, it might be worth the investment to streamline your review collection process and build a more consistent reviewer base.

Once you've tapped into platforms like Booksprout for those impactful early reviews, it's time to consider more organic approaches. One of the most effective, yet often overlooked, methods is leveraging social media, particularly Facebook groups. This strategy can take a bit more time and effort, but it offers the potential for long-term connections and ongoing reader support, which can be invaluable as you continue to publish more books.

Using Social Media and Facebook Groups

Social media can be a powerful tool for gathering reviews, especially if your book targets a niche with active online communities. Facebook, in particular, is a goldmine for this, with thousands of groups dedicated to nearly every topic imaginable. If you've written a book on container gardening, for instance, you might join groups like "Container Gardening Enthusiasts" or "Small Space Gardeners," where members are already deeply interested in your subject.

It's also crucial to avoid coming across as overly promotional or spammy in these groups. Most have strict rules against self-promotion, and if you're too aggressive, you risk being banned, which would undo all the effort you've put into building your credibility. Instead, aim to add genuine value to the conversations, share helpful insights, and only mention your book when it feels natural and appropriate. For example, if someone asks about the best soil for container gardening, you might share a few insights from your book. This builds trust and credibility, making other members more likely to support you when you eventually mention your book.

Additionally, consider reaching out directly to group admins before promoting your book. If you have a genuinely valuable resource, like a detailed container gardening guide, the admin might be open to sharing it with the group. Many admins are passionate about providing quality content to their members and may even be willing to pin your post or feature it in the group's announcements, giving you a significant visibility boost. When making this approach, emphasize the specific value your book offers to the group's members, like exclusive tips or strategies they won't find in generic online articles.

Once you've established some credibility, take the next step by directly messaging individual members who have shown interest in your topic. This is where you can offer them a free digital copy of your book in exchange for an honest review. For an even more personal touch, consider adding them as friends before reaching out. People are far more likely to respond positively to someone they feel they've had a genuine interaction with, rather than a random stranger.

While this approach can be highly effective, it's important to remember that it's also a numbers game. Not everyone you message will respond, and even fewer will actually take the time to leave a review. In my experience, and that of other authors I know, the typical success rate ranges from 10-30%. This means that if you reach out to 100 people, you might realistically expect 10 to 30 reviews. This might sound discouraging, but when you consider that each review adds social proof and boosts your book's credibility, the effort is well worth it.

Don't get discouraged if this process feels slow at first. Building a solid base of reviews is one of the most impactful things you can do for your book's long-term success. Every genuine review you earn is a small but powerful piece of social proof that can make all the difference in converting curious browsers into paying customers. Keep pushing, keep engaging, and over time, those reviews will start to add up.

Using Pubby and Similar Review Platforms

Another option for gathering reviews is using platforms like Pubby, a paid service ($29/month) designed specifically to help self-published authors get more Amazon reviews. Pubby operates on a credit-based system, where you earn credits (called "snaps") by reading and reviewing other authors' books. You can then use these credits to request reviews for your own books, creating a community-driven review exchange.

Here's how Pubby works. Once you sign up, you upload your book to the platform and make it available for review. You earn snaps (Pubby's internal credit system) by reading and reviewing other authors' books. You can then spend those snaps to get reviews for your own book, creating an indirect, community-driven exchange that stays compliant with Amazon's guidelines.

The number of snaps required for a review is determined by several factors: your book's Kindle price, its length, whether you're requesting a verified or unverified review, and how quickly you want the review to be completed. Higher-priced books, faster turnaround times, or verified reviews will typically cost more snaps. This flexible system helps keep things balanced and fair, while still making it possible to generate reviews consistently over time.

It's still a solid option for building those first few critical reviews, especially if you're just starting out. Just be sure to leave honest, balanced feedback when reviewing others' work, as this not only builds your credibility within the platform but also helps you avoid potential issues with Amazon's algorithm, which can flag accounts that only leave glowing, five-star reviews.

If you're looking for alternatives to Pubby, there are a few other platforms worth considering. Sites like Hidden Gems, Reading Deals, and BookSirens connect authors with readers willing to leave honest reviews.

Bringing It All Together

To maximize the impact of your reviews, it's best to use a combination of all these approaches. Platforms like Booksprout can help you gather those vital early reviews, while social media groups provide a steady trickle of ongoing feedback from highly engaged readers. Pubby and similar platforms can fill in the gaps, helping you consistently add new reviews as your book gains traction.

When reaching out to readers, don't be afraid to ask for the highest-value reviews, like those with photos or even video, as these carry the most weight in terms of social proof. Just keep in mind that not everyone will be willing or able to do this, so be flexible. The important thing is to make the process as easy as possible, whether that's through a quick follow-up email, a friendly direct message, or a simple call to action at the end of your book.

In the end, building a diverse portfolio of reviews will give your book the best chance of long-term success on Amazon, helping it climb the rankings, attract more organic traffic, and convert more browsers into buyers. Keep experimenting, stay patient, and remember that every review, no matter how small, contributes to your book's credibility and sales potential.

18

AUDIOBOOKS

Audiobooks are no longer just a nice extra—they're a fast-growing format that opens your book up to an entirely new audience. As more people consume content while driving, walking, or multitasking, the demand for audio continues to rise. The global market is projected to reach $39.1 billion by 2032, and that growth means opportunity. Audiobooks also offer an inclusive way to reach listeners with reading difficulties or visual impairments—people who might not engage with your book otherwise. And with smartphones, smart speakers, and wireless earbuds now part of everyday life, accessing audiobooks has never been easier. For self-publishers, offering your book in audio isn't just about keeping up—it's about expanding your reach, increasing your royalties, and making your content more accessible to everyone.

Where to Publish Your Audiobook

If you're ready to turn your book into an audiobook, the next step is choosing where to publish it. The best place to start is with the platform that dominates the market: Audible. If you're in the U.S., U.K., or Canada, publishing directly through ACX.com (the backend platform for Audible, Amazon, and iTunes) is the most effective route. It follows the 80/20 rule—giving you the biggest return for the least complexity.

Royalty Options on ACX

When publishing your audiobook through ACX, you have several payment models to choose from—and the one you select can significantly affect both your upfront costs and long-term royalties. Understanding these options is especially important if you're just starting out and need to manage your cash flow wisely.

1. Per Finished Hour (PFH)

This is the most straightforward model. You pay your narrator a fixed rate for every hour of the final, edited audio—regardless of how long it actually takes them to record or produce it. For example, if your audiobook ends up being 3.5 hours long and the narrator charges $60 PFH, you'll pay $210 total.

Rates vary widely, from $40 to over $400 per finished hour, depending on the narrator's experience and audio quality. For most self-publishers, the sweet spot tends to fall between $40–$100 PFH, where you can balance affordability with decent production value.

With PFH, you retain full rights to your audiobook and keep 100% of your royalties—that means 40% of every sale if you choose exclusive distribution, or 25% if you go non-exclusive. Exclusive distribution means your audiobook will only be available through Audible, Amazon, and iTunes, but you'll earn a higher royalty rate. Non-exclusive distribution allows you to sell your audiobook on other platforms as well but at a lower royalty rate.

PFH gives you complete control over your audiobook and where it's sold, but it does require an upfront investment.

2. Royalty Share

With this model, you don't pay anything upfront. Instead, you split your audiobook royalties 50/50 with the narrator. You each earn 20% of every sale (Audible keeps the remaining 60%). This is a great option if you don't have much money to spend but still want to get your audiobook out there. Just keep in mind—narrators are selective. They'll only accept a royalty share deal if your book has strong potential. That usually means it already has a solid number of reviews and steady sales on Amazon or Kindle.

3. Royalty Share Plus

This is a hybrid model where you offer a smaller upfront payment and still split royalties 50/50. This gives you a better shot at attracting high-quality narrators who want some guaranteed payment, but are still willing to take a chance on your book's future success. It's a great compromise if you don't have the full **PFH** budget but want to secure a better narrator than you might get with a standard royalty share.

Both royalty share models are only available if you choose exclusive distribution. You'll earn a higher royalty rate (40%), but your audiobook will be limited to Audible, Amazon, and iTunes.

If you prefer broader reach, you'll need to go non-exclusive. This lowers your royalty rate to 25%, but gives you the freedom to distribute your audiobook on other platforms, like Findaway Voices (which I'll cover in the next section). Non-exclusive makes more sense once you've built a few audiobooks and want to expand your audience, but exclusive is usually the better option for beginners thanks to the higher royalties and access to ACX's royalty-share features.

In short:

- **PFH** gives you full rights and control but requires upfront payment; you earn 40% (exclusive) or 25% (non-exclusive).

- **Royalty Share** gives you zero upfront cost, but you split royalties 50/50 and must publish exclusively.

- **Royalty Share Plus** lets you pay less upfront while still sharing royalties —ideal for mid-budget authors seeking quality.

Expanded Distribution with Findaway Voices

While ACX is the go-to platform for publishing to Audible, Amazon, and iTunes, it's not available to authors outside the U.S., U.K., Canada, and Ireland. And even if you are eligible, there may come a time when you want to expand beyond those three retailers. That's where Findaway Voices comes in.

Findaway Voices (often referred to as FV) is a powerful platform that distributes your audiobook to over 40 additional retailers and libraries, including Spotify, Apple Books, Chirp, Kobo, Google Play, Scribd, Storytel, and many others. It's a great way to diversify your income streams and reach listeners who prefer alternatives to Audible—or live in countries where Audible isn't dominant.

If you choose the non-exclusive option on ACX, you're free to upload your audiobook to Findaway Voices as well. This gives you access to both the biggest platform (Audible) and dozens of other listening apps around the world. While the royalty rate on ACX drops to 25% under non-exclusive, the tradeoff is wider exposure and long-term diversification.

Findaway also allows for more pricing flexibility. While Audible sets pricing automatically, Findaway lets you set your own retail price, which gives you more control over promotions and limited-time discounts (especially if you're using Chirp Deals or other promo tools). They also have a marketplace for narrators similar to ACX, so if you're not happy with your narrator options on one platform, you can explore the other.

It's worth noting that Findaway was acquired by Spotify in 2022, which gives it even greater long-term potential as Spotify continues to push into the audiobook space.

If you're just starting out and your main goal is simplicity and maximum royalties, exclusive ACX is usually the best choice. But if you're publishing from outside an ACX-supported country, or if you already have a few audiobooks under your belt and want to expand, Findaway

Voices is the logical next step. It gives you more control, more reach, and a bigger slice of the growing audio pie.

Optimizing Length for Maximum Royalties

One of the most overlooked aspects of audiobook planning is choosing the right book length to maximize your earnings. Unlike eBooks, where pricing is up to you, Audible sets the retail price of your audiobook based on the total runtime—not the word count. That means even a relatively short book can earn solid royalties if it falls into the right length bracket.

Here's how Audible royalties generally break down:

- 1 to 3 hours of audio earns you roughly $3 per sale
- 3 to 5 hours earns about $7 per sale
- 5 to 10 hours brings in around $10 per sale

Audiobook Length	Retail Price	Net Sales $
< 1hr	3.95	2.05
1-3 hrs	6.95	3.61
3-5 hrs	14.95	7.77
5-10 hrs	19.95	10.37
10-20 hrs	24.95	12.97
20 hrs +	29.95	15.57

Knowing this, the "sweet spot" for most first-time audiobook creators is 3 hours. Why? It hits that $7 royalty tier while keeping production costs lower than a longer, 10-hour project. To get into that range, aim for a manuscript of about 30,000 words. That's typically enough to produce 3 hours of finished audio, assuming a standard reading pace.

A common mistake new authors make is underestimating the word count needed to hit that 3-hour minimum. On average, 27,000 spoken words result in about 3 hours of audio, so targeting 30,000 words gives you a safe buffer. It's a smart idea to discuss this with your narrator upfront so they can pace their reading appropriately and ensure the finished product lands in your ideal range. Nothing's worse than planning for a $7 royalty tier and ending up just short.

Whether you're self-narrating or hiring a professional, keep runtime in mind. It affects your earnings, your production budget, and ultimately how competitive your audiobook will be in the Audible marketplace.

Choosing the Right Narrator

A narrator can make or break your audiobook. The right voice doesn't just read your words—it brings them to life. A warm, confident tone can build trust in a nonfiction guide. A dramatic delivery can elevate the tension in a thriller. Even a basic how-to book becomes more engaging when read clearly, with the right pacing and energy.

Before hiring anyone, take a few minutes to think about what kind of voice best fits your content. Ask yourself:

• Should the narrator be male or female?

• Do you want a calm, instructional tone—or something more energetic and dynamic?

• If it's fiction, will different characters need distinct voices or accents?

• Would a particular accent help (or hurt) your book's appeal to your audience?

• How fast do you need the project completed?

• Are you paying per finished hour or offering a royalty share deal?

Most authors find their narrators on ACX, where they're called "producers." That's because they don't just record your book—they edit and master it into a retail-ready audiobook. You can either browse voice samples based on criteria like gender, age, accent, and vocal style—or create an open audition, where narrators submit a custom sample from your script.

If your book is in a niche like self-help, language learning, or finance, clarity and professionalism should be your top priority. If you're writing fiction or a memoir, you'll want someone who can deliver emotion, pacing, and even perform multiple voices when needed.

Keep in mind: narrators are in demand. Many top-tier voices are booked out weeks or months in advance, and they're selective about the projects they accept—especially for royalty share deals. That's why it helps to have solid sales or positive reviews on your Kindle or paperback version first. A proven track record increases your odds of attracting a great narrator, even without a huge budget.

Once you've narrowed your choices, don't be afraid to hop on a Zoom call or message back and forth to align on expectations. Discuss pacing, tone, how you want certain sections delivered, and how long the project will take. A good narrator will be open to collaboration and committed to helping your book sound its best.

Recording the Audiobook Yourself

If you're comfortable speaking into a microphone and want to stay hands-on with your book, you might consider narrating the audiobook yourself. It's a tempting option for many first-time authors—especially if you're working with a tight budget or writing nonfiction where your voice can actually deepen the connection with listeners.

There are definite advantages. You have total creative control. You don't need to pay a narrator, and for memoirs or certain how-to books, hearing the author's actual voice can add authenticity and trust. If your readers already connect with you through your writing, your voice might be the thing that makes the audiobook feel even more personal.

That said, it's not always as simple as hitting "record." Narrating a high-quality audiobook requires time, patience, and the right setup. At a minimum, you'll need a decent microphone, some basic soundproofing (like recording in a quiet closet or using acoustic foam panels), and audio editing software to clean up mistakes and background noise.

A few tools worth checking out:

• Audacity (free, beginner-friendly editing software)

• Reaper (a more advanced but affordable option for long-term use)

• Auphonic (great for leveling and mastering your audio automatically)

You'll also need to factor in time—not just to record, but to edit and master the audio to meet ACX's technical requirements. It's not impossible, but it does take effort. If you're not already familiar with audio production, expect a learning curve.

Generally, I only recommend DIY narration in two cases:

1. You're writing nonfiction and want to connect directly with your audience.

2. You're confident in your speaking voice and willing to learn basic audio editing.

Even then, you might consider hiring a professional to do the final mastering to ensure your files meet ACX's standards. Nothing's worse than spending hours recording your audiobook, only to have it rejected for technical reasons.

If you're unsure, try narrating a single chapter and playing it back as if you were a customer. Ask yourself: Would I want to listen to this for 3–5 hours? If the answer is yes—and you're enjoying the process—then go for it.

Otherwise, hiring a narrator might be a better investment of your time and energy, especially as your publishing income grows.

My Reflections

If you're just beginning your self-publishing journey, it's probably not the best idea to dive into audiobooks right away. Instead, I recommend focusing on writing and publishing a few solid books first. This will give you the chance to understand the basics, refine your writing skills, and gain a better grasp of the publishing process.

Once your books start generating a steady monthly income—say, around $500—you'll have a bit more financial breathing room to invest in audiobooks. This strategy also makes sense from a cash flow perspective, as you can use the profits from your eBook and paperback sales to cover the cost of narration.

For a 30,000-word book, you can expect to pay $120-$240 for basic narration, depending on the experience of the narrator and the quality of the final production ($40-$80 per finished hour of narration). By waiting until you have a few profitable books under your belt, you'll be better positioned to expand into audiobooks without stretching your budget too thin.

19

PRICING YOUR BOOKS

Setting the right price for your books isn't just about maximizing profit—it's also about making them attractive to potential buyers. Striking the right balance between affordability and profitability is key to building a successful self-publishing business.

Pricing Low-Content Books

Low-content books like journals, planners, coloring books, and activity books are typically priced between $3.99 and $9.99. The sweet spot is around $6.99, which usually results in a $2 profit per sale. It's tough to sell these books for much more, given the intense competition and the abundance of similar, high-quality options available. This is one of the main reasons why I generally suggest steering clear of these types of books.

Pricing Fiction Books

If you're considering writing fiction, it's important to understand how pricing works in this genre. Unlike nonfiction, fiction books are generally priced lower, whether they're self-published or traditionally published. For example, a bestselling hardcover might start at $19.99, but it often drops to $9.99 or even $6.99 for the paperback version. eBooks, on the other hand, can be priced as low as $0.99 to $2.99, making them highly competitive.

For self-published authors, it's unrealistic to price a first fiction book at $20 or even $10, as the focus should be on gaining visibility, building an audience, and collecting those essential early reviews. Enrolling your book in Kindle Select can be a smart move, as it increases your chances of being discovered by Kindle Unlimited readers, providing a steady trickle of page-read royalties.

The reason fiction books tend to have lower prices is because the market is much larger, with avid readers often consuming multiple books a week. Additionally, many self-published fiction authors produce shorter books more frequently, with lengths as short as 30,000 words compared to the 80,000+ word counts typically seen in traditionally published novels.

Pricing Nonfiction Books

Nonfiction books generally command higher prices than fiction because they often provide specialized knowledge, practical advice, or unique insights. Readers are typically willing to pay more for well-researched, authoritative content, making this a more lucrative category.

When pricing your nonfiction book, consider factors like your target audience, the competitive landscape, and the perceived value of your content. Research similar titles in your niche to get a sense of what readers are willing to pay. Personally, I price my nonfiction books between $12.99 and $19.99, depending on the competition and the number of reviews.

A smart way to find the ideal price point is to start on the lower end and gradually increase the price. For example, you can raise it by a dollar every two weeks and monitor your sales. If they stay steady, you can continue adjusting the price upward until you notice a decline, which likely indicates you've hit the upper limit of what readers are willing to pay.

Hardcovers

When pricing hardcovers, I generally set them about $10 higher than the paperback version. There are a few reasons for this approach:

First, hardcovers are more expensive to produce, so a higher price is necessary to maintain a similar profit margin. If you price your paperback at $14.99, for example, it makes sense to set the hardcover at $24.99 or $29.99 to account for these higher production costs.

Second, this strategy takes advantage of a psychological concept called price anchoring. This is the idea that the presence of a higher-priced option makes the lower-priced item seem like a better deal. For instance, if a hardcover is listed at $29.99 and the paperback is $19.99, the paperback feels like a more attractive option by comparison, even if it's still priced on the higher end.

Lastly, some readers simply prefer hardcovers and are willing to pay the premium. These buyers appreciate the sturdiness, collectible nature, and presentation of hardcovers, making it easier to justify the higher price. At $24.99 or $29.99, you can earn royalties of $10 or more per sale, which can significantly boost your overall profits.

In short, pricing your hardcovers higher not only covers the production costs but also leverages price anchoring to make your paperbacks look like a better deal, while capturing sales from readers who prefer the premium format.

20

MARKETING & SOCIAL MEDIA

Over the years, I've tried various marketing strategies to promote my books, and I've learned a few things along the way. Early on, I leaned into Instagram as my main platform, even growing an account to over 200,000 followers for one of my brands. However, I quickly realized that the time and effort spent managing a social media account could have been better used for writing more books. Daily posting, content creation, and constant engagement became a drain, and the sales generated didn't justify the workload.

I also experimented with Facebook ads, but found the costs high and the returns disappointing. The multi-step process of capturing attention, encouraging a click, leading someone to Amazon, and converting that click into a sale proved challenging. The conversion rates just didn't add up, and it felt like a distraction from my main goal—creating quality books.

From my experience, traditional social media marketing isn't the most efficient approach for selling books. While some authors have found success with it, I believe the time, money, and mental energy required could be better spent elsewhere.

Instead, I recommend focusing on a strategy that truly aligns with the 80/20 rule—collecting emails. This approach provides a direct line to your readers, allowing you to notify them about future releases, request reviews, and build a loyal audience over time.

Here's how it works: include a QR code or a simple link at the back of your book, inviting readers to sign up for a free bonus, like a downloadable guide or exclusive content. Once your book starts selling, you'll automatically start collecting emails, creating a valuable asset that you can leverage for future launches.

For email collection, I use ConvertKit. At the time of this writing, it's free to collect your first 1,000 emails, making it a cost-effective way to start building your list. They also offer a range of tutorials on how to set up simple email opt-ins, so you can get started without much hassle.

The key is to offer a "lead magnet"—a small, valuable freebie that entices readers to share their email. This could be anything from a bonus chapter to a printable worksheet, depending on your niche. Once set up, this system runs in the background, collecting emails and building your audience while you focus on writing your next book.

Here are a few ideas based on different book categories:

Health and Fitness

• 7-Day Meal Plan – A simple, downloadable guide for a week of healthy eating.

• Home Workout Routine – A PDF or video series for a quick, effective home workout.

Personal Development

• Goal-Setting Worksheet – A fillable worksheet to help people set and achieve their goals.

- Daily Planner Template – A printable planner to keep readers organized and focused.

Finance

- Budget Tracker Spreadsheet – A downloadable spreadsheet to help manage personal finances.
- Investment Cheat Sheet – A quick guide to understanding basic investment strategies.

Business and Marketing

- Social Media Content Calendar – A pre-made calendar to streamline social media planning.
- Email Marketing Templates – A set of pre-written emails for different stages of a sales funnel.

Travel

- Packing Checklist – A printable checklist for different types of trips.
- Travel Savings Guide – Tips and tricks for saving money while traveling.

The key to a successful lead magnet is to make it highly relevant to your audience, easy to consume, and instantly valuable. It should solve a specific problem or address a common pain point, while also showcasing your expertise. This not only builds trust but also sets the stage for future book sales.

21

AMAZON ADS FOR AUTHORS

When it comes to selling books, it makes sense to target customers who are already on Amazon and actively looking to make a purchase. That's why I focus my advertising efforts solely on Amazon's own platform.

It might seem strange to pay for ads on the same platform where your books are sold, but the reality is that you're competing with thousands of other titles. Unless your book is an instant bestseller, running ads is often necessary to gain visibility and drive sales.

According to Amazon, 30% of readers browse the platform specifically to find books, and 65% discover new titles while shopping on the site. This means that a significant portion of your potential audience is already primed to make a purchase, making Amazon ads a powerful tool for reaching new readers.

Different Advertising Methods

When it comes to promoting your books on Amazon, the platform offers three main types of ads, each with its own strengths and use cases:

Sponsored Product Ads: These are the most common and effective ads for self-published authors. They operate on a cost-per-click (CPC) model, meaning you only pay when someone clicks on your ad. Sponsored Product Ads appear on search results pages and individual product pages, giving your book prime visibility. You can control your daily budget and set a maximum bid per click, making it easier to manage costs. This is a great starting point, as it allows you to target specific keywords or categories related to your book.

Sponsored Brand Ads: These ads also follow a CPC model but are designed for authors with multiple books or a well-defined brand. They showcase your brand logo, a custom headline, and several products, typically appearing at the top or bottom of search results pages. If you have a series or a collection of related books, this can be a powerful way to drive brand recognition and boost sales across multiple titles. However, these ads require a bit more planning and budget than Sponsored Product Ads.

Lockscreen Ads: These ads are exclusive to U.S. publishers and appear on the lock screens of Kindle e-readers and Fire tablets. While this might sound appealing, they tend to be more expensive and less effective for self-published authors. Personally, I avoid these ads, as they often target a less engaged audience. As a Kindle owner myself, I rarely notice these ads, and many readers, like me, disable them altogether.

For most self-published authors, I recommend starting with Sponsored Product Ads, as they are simpler to manage and can deliver strong results. Once you've seen some success, you can consider experimenting with Sponsored Brand Ads.

Getting Started with Ads

To start advertising your book on Amazon, the first step is to create an account at advertising.amazon.com. The process is straightforward and free, though you'll need to add a payment method like a credit or debit card to cover your ad spend. Alternatively, you can set up a bank account for direct withdrawals. Once your account is active, you're ready to launch your first ad campaign.

After logging into the Amazon Advertising dashboard, you'll see a "Create campaign" button, which will guide you through the setup process. You'll have three main options: Sponsored Products, Sponsored Brands, and Lockscreen Ads. For beginners, Sponsored Products is the best choice, so go ahead and click that option to get started.

The first step is to select an ad format. You'll have two choices: Custom text ads or Standard ads. Custom text ads allow you to add a short message along with your book cover, which can be a good choice for fiction books or highly competitive niches. Standard ads display just your book cover, star rating, and price, which can be effective for nonfiction books where the cover alone clearly communicates the book's content. For this example, it's simpler to start with the Standard ad option, as it often performs well for both fiction and nonfiction titles.

Next, you'll need to pick the book you want to advertise. If you have Kindle, paperback, and hardcover versions, it might seem like a good idea to run ads for all three, but it's usually more effective to focus on the paperback. This is because the paperback price is typically positioned between the lower-cost eBook and the premium-priced hardcover, striking a balance that attracts a broader range of buyers while still providing a solid return on ad spend. Potential buyers can see the price before clicking, reducing the risk of wasting money on clicks that don't convert. Advertising a $2.99 Kindle eBook can quickly become unprofitable, as the profit margin is much smaller. As for hardcovers, they tend to attract a smaller, more selective audience, which can make ads less cost-effective. For this reason, paperbacks generally strike a better balance between affordability for buyers and profitability for you as the author.

After selecting your book, you'll be asked to choose between Automatic and Manual targeting. For beginners, Automatic Targeting is a good starting point. With this option, Amazon's algorithm will automatically match your ad to relevant keywords and products based on the content of your book. It's a great way to let Amazon do the heavy lifting while you get a feel for how the system works. Once you gain more experience, you can switch to Manual Targeting for greater control. This approach allows you to handpick the specific keywords or product categories where you want your ad to appear, which can lead to more precise targeting and potentially lower costs over time.

Next, you'll need to decide how much you're willing to pay each time someone clicks on your ad. You'll see a "Suggested bid" range, but it's usually better to choose a Custom bid instead. The suggested bids are often too high, especially when you're just starting out. Instead, try entering a low, odd-numbered bid like 21 cents or 31 cents. This small detail can make your ad more competitive, as most advertisers tend to stick with even numbers.

Once you've set your initial bid, you can let your auto ad run to gather some data and get a feel for how the system works. After a few days or weeks, you'll start to see which keywords are performing well and where your budget is being effectively spent. At this point, you might be ready to take more control with manual targeting.

This brings you to the choice between two main targeting options: Keyword targeting and Product targeting. Keyword targeting allows you to choose specific words and phrases that potential customers might use when searching for books like yours on Amazon. You can either create your own keyword list, rely on Amazon's suggested keywords, or use a mix of both. Meanwhile, Product targeting lets you directly aim your ads at particular products, categories, or brands, which can be a useful strategy if you want your book to appear alongside similar titles or complementary products. Both approaches have their strengths, so it's worth experimenting to find what works best for your specific book and niche.

After setting your bid rate, you'll move on to selecting keywords. Amazon offers three main keyword types: broad, phrase, and exact. Broad keywords give Amazon the flexibility to match your ads with a wide range of related search terms, including similar words, synonyms, misspellings, and variations. For example, if you choose "Ketogenic Cookbook" as a broad keyword, your ad might show up for searches like "Keto cookbook," "Ketogenic Cookbooks," or even common spelling errors like "Ketogeniccookbook."

Phrase keywords are a bit more precise, targeting search terms that include your exact keyword in any order. So, if you use "Ketogenic Cookbook" as a phrase keyword, your ad could appear for searches like "Vegan Ketogenic Cookbook" or "Ketogenic Cookbook for beginners."

Exact keywords are the most focused, only matching your ad with search terms that precisely match your chosen keyword. If you select "Ketogenic Cookbook" as an exact keyword, your ad will only show up for that specific search phrase, without any extra words before or after it.

When you're just getting started, it's often a good idea to select all three types. Amazon generally pre-selects them by default, which can be a helpful starting point. Over time, as you gather more data on what works best for your book, you might choose to focus on one or two of these keyword types for better targeting.

After choosing your keywords, you'll come to the negative keyword targeting section. This is an optional, yet valuable step that allows you to exclude certain search terms from triggering your ads. For instance, if you've written a book on personal finance for teenagers, you might want to prevent your ad from appearing in searches like "personal finance for adults" or "retirement finance," as those audiences aren't your ideal readers. Keeping a document with a list of negative keywords for each of your books can make this process quicker when setting up new campaigns. Just be sure to enter these terms as both negative exact and negative phrase to ensure they're fully excluded from your targeting.

Campaigns

The next section you'll encounter is the Campaign settings, where you'll select your campaign bidding strategy. Amazon offers three main options here. The first is dynamic bids—down only, which allows Amazon to reduce your bids in real-time if it detects a lower chance of a sale, helping you control costs. The second option is dynamic bids—up and down, where Amazon will both increase and decrease your bids as needed, potentially raising them by up to 100% if a sale seems likely, while still lowering them if the chances are slim. The final option is fixed bids, where your bid remains exactly as you've set it, without any automatic adjustments from Amazon. Personally, I prefer the down-only approach, as it provides a bit more control over ad spending without risking unexpectedly high costs.

Next, you'll need to name your campaign. This can be as simple as the title of your book, or you can use a more descriptive name if you plan to run multiple ads for the same title. My usual format is "Book name - manual/PA (product ad)/auto," like "Ketogenic (manual)" or "Ketogenic (auto)." This keeps things organized and helps you quickly identify each campaign in your dashboard.

As for the start and end dates, the default is to start the campaign immediately on the day you create it, with no set end date. I recommend leaving the end date open and simply pausing or stopping the ad when necessary, rather than setting a fixed end date upfront. This approach gives you more flexibility and prevents your ads from accidentally turning off just as they're starting to gain momentum.

The marketplace setting is usually pre-selected based on your account location, which for most authors will be the United States. This is a good place to start, as the U.S. remains the largest and most profitable Amazon market. Once you have a book consistently earning around $500 per month, you might consider expanding to other markets like the U.K., Canada, or Australia.

Finally, set your daily budget. A good starting point is $5, which keeps your initial investment manageable while you test the waters. If your ad starts performing well, you can always increase this amount later. Once you've reviewed all your settings, you can either save the campaign as a draft or click the "Launch campaign" button to set it live. Don't worry if you make a mistake or want to tweak your approach later—you can always go back and adjust your ads as needed.

22

CONCLUSION

The self-publishing world is a playground for aspiring authors. It's where you can take control of your creative journey, free from the constraints of traditional publishing. You get to make decisions on everything from the content to the cover, and most importantly, you get to keep a bigger share of the profits. But it's not just about writing your ideas down. There's a practical side to it that involves getting the formatting right, designing a cover that grabs attention, and setting up a marketing strategy that works. It takes time and effort, but with the guidance in this book, you'll be well-equipped to navigate the self-publishing path and make it financially rewarding.

When I look back at my own experience, I realize that out of my first ten books, only one became a hit, consistently making over $1,000 a month. That's something to keep in mind as you start out. It might take several tries before you find success, and that's perfectly normal. The key is not to give up. As long as you keep pushing forward, your chances of hitting the mark increase. The aim of this book is to help you avoid the mistakes I made, giving you a faster and more efficient route to success and financial growth.

One of the best ways to stay motivated and informed is by connecting with the self-publishing community. You'll find valuable advice from experienced authors in Facebook groups, YouTube channels, and other online spaces. These communities are full of people sharing tips, strategies, and the latest industry insights. Staying updated is crucial since the self-publishing landscape keeps evolving.

Success in self-publishing often follows the principle of "write, publish, repeat." The more books you put out, the better your chances of making consistent income and growing your author career. Every new book helps you improve as a writer, refine your cover design skills, and streamline your publishing process. By sharing the lessons I've learned, I hope to make your journey smoother and more successful.

To sum it all up, here's what makes a successful book:

• Finding a keyword that will make your book profitable.

• Outlining the structure of your book.

• Writing the content yourself or hiring a ghostwriter.

• Editing your manuscript or using an editor to polish it.

• Formatting the book for publishing or hiring a professional formatter.

• Designing a compelling cover or hiring a designer.

• Uploading your book in eBook, paperback, and hardcover formats on KDP.

• Collecting early reviews to build credibility and drive conversions.

• Setting up effective ads to boost visibility and sales.

Now it's your turn. Start writing, publish your book, and take advantage of Amazon KDP to turn your passion into profit.

And while you do, I'd love to hear how this guide helped you along the way. If you have a moment, it would mean a lot if you could share your thoughts on this book by leaving a review. It not only helps other aspiring authors find this guide, but it also supports me in continuing to share what I've learned on this journey. Your feedback is incredibly valuable, and I truly appreciate every word. Just scan the QR code below to head straight to the review page. Thank you!

All Links

KDP account creation

kdp.amazon.com/signin

Keyword research software

https://www.kdspy.com/

BSR viewer

https://chrome.google.com/webstore/detail/ds-amazon-quick-view/jkompbllimaoekaogchhkmkdogpkhojg

Pen name generator

https://blog.reedsy.com/pen-name-generator/

Paperback cover generator

https://kdp.amazon.com/en_US/cover-calculator

Design software

www.canva.com

Email marketing software

https://app.convertkit.com/users/signup?plan=free-limited&lmref=Lz6sJQ

Amazon advertising

http://advertising.amazon.com

100 Covers

https://100covers.com/

Upwork

https://www.upwork.com/

Fiverr

https://www.fiverr.com/

Booksprout

https://booksprout.co/

If you want all the links on one neatly organized clickable PDF, scan the QR code, enter your email and I'll send it to you!

www.ingramcontent.com/pod-product-compliance
Lightning Source LLC
Chambersburg PA
CBHW071208070526
44584CB00019B/2963